E ighteen-year-old Regina McBride is haunted by the ghosts of her parents. Her father visits her—he is desperate, but she doesn't know how to help him. Her mother is a quiet figure, obscured by light—a flash at the foot of the bed. Regina, raised Irish Catholic and with the ironclad belief that some sins are unforgivable, fears her parents are trapped between worlds, forever punished after they committed suicide within a few months of each other.

Terrorized by these visitations and flattened by grief, Regina slowly begins her hazardous journey to recovery. Lyrical and lovely, harrowing and haunting, *Ghost Songs* charts her struggle to separate madness from imagination and sorrow from devastation. From New York to the desert of New Mexico to the shores of Ireland, Regina searches for herself, her home, and a way to return to the family that remains. *Ghost Songs* is an exploration of memory, a meditation on love and loss, and, in the end, a celebration of life and the living.

PRAISE FOR *Ghost Songs*

"In Regina McBride's *Ghost Songs* there is a mysterious alchemy at play. With a subtle hand, McBride transforms personal horror into poetic myth. In writing this story that happened to her in real time, she creates a book that feels timeless. I was under its spell from word one."

—ALICE SEBOLD, author of *Lucky*

"Dubbed a literary Maeve Binchy by an LJ reviewer for her affecting, lyrical fiction (e.g., *The Nature of Water and Air*), McBride will make you sit up straight with this startling memoir, grounded in singular sorrow: her parents committed suicide one after the other when she was only seventeen. McBride's subsequent hunt for comfort and belonging took her from New York to New Mexico to Ireland, where she reconnected with her roots and the gorgeous Irish lore that informs her writing. Yet she still had to contend with the painful recognition that Catholicism regards suicides as unpardonable sin."

—*Library Journal*, Barbara Hoffert

"It's a wonder to me that after reading this book of such intense pain and deep sorrow that I felt—and know I'll continue to feel—peace and hope. Regina McBride has written a beautiful memoir in which ghosts—individual and compound—can, like the living, be transformed from that which we fear to that which we might accept and love."

—MICHAEL THOMAS, author of *Man Gone Down*, winner of the International IMPAC Dublin Award

GHOST
SONGS

GHOST SONGS

a memoir

Regina McBride

Tin House Books
Portland, Oregon & Brooklyn, New York

Copyright © 2016 Regina McBride

Published by Tin House Books, Portland, Oregon and Brooklyn, New York

Distributed by W. W. Norton and Company.

Library of Congress Cataloging-in-Publication Data
Names: McBride, Regina, 1956- author.
Title: Ghost songs : a memoir / Regina McBride.
Description: 1st U.S. edition. | Portland, OR : Tin House Books, 2016.
Identifiers: LCCN 2016006743 (print) | LCCN 2016018549 (ebook) | ISBN
   9781941040430 (pbk. : alk. paper) | ISBN 9781941040447
Subjects: LCSH: McBride, Regina, 1956- | Authors, American--20th
   century--Biography.
Classification: LCC PS3563.C333628 Z46 2016 (print) | LCC PS3563.C333628
   (ebook) | DDC 813/.54 [B] --dc23
LC record available at https://lccn.loc.gov/2016006743

First US edition 2016
Printed in the USA
Interior design by Diane Chonette
www.tinhouse.com

For Jerry, Tracy, and Sheila—with love

The host is riding from Knocknarea
And over the grave of Clooth-na-Bare;
Caoilte tossing his burning hair,
And Niamh calling *Away, come away:*
Empty your heart of its mortal dream.

—W. B. YEATS, "The Hosting of the Sidhe"

You are Irish you say lightly, and allocated to you are
the tendencies to be wild, wanton, drunk, superstitious,
unreliable, backward, toadying and prone to fits,
whereas you know that in fact a whole entourage of
ghosts resides in you, ghosts with whom the inner
rapport is as frequent, as perplexing, as defiant as with
any of the living.

—EDNA O'BRIEN, *Mother Ireland: A Memoir*

PART ONE

A particular memory preoccupies me. A theater party in Santa Fe. I don't know many people and walk to the back patio, where, in the porch light, two young actors are reciting lines from Shakespeare. Turning and seeing me standing at the open French doors, one of them goes down on his knee and bows to me. The other kisses my hand and in an impassioned whisper utters, "My lady Ophelia." The two of them fence for me with rapiers of air.

I lie in the sterile psychiatric ward, playing and replaying this memory. In my mind I wear a long green velvet dress and flowers in my hair. I feel bright lights on my face and gesture out into the darkness of my audience.

•

I hear breathing, a dry broken noise like fabric dragging on rough wood. On the wall in my hospital room, something shimmers in the afternoon light. It is my father. I sit up and avert my eyes and he becomes more defined, as if he is meant to be seen from the far side of the eye, where apparitions live.

The air is mineral-heavy, like it might rain inside the room. A sharp, sweet odor deepens around me—garbage and rotten apples. Sitting on the edge of the bed, I collapse forward, close my eyes, and hold my breath against the smell—but I can't hide from the sound, a dry struggle to breathe. My father is lost and doesn't know where to go.

•

I lean against the headboard of my bed in near darkness, looking across the hall into my parents' room where the bedside lamp is on. I must be almost five years old because we are in the new house in New Mexico. My parents are getting ready for bed, my mother wearing a white nightgown with no sleeves and my father with his shirt off.

They face each other, standing close whispering so they don't wake my baby sister, Sheila, whose crib is near their dresser. With a finger, my father gently moves my mother's hair away from her temple. She says something and they stifle a laugh. They kiss and my mother rests the side of her face against his chest.

My father sees me watching and tells her. She comes in very quietly so she doesn't wake my little sister Tracy, who is sleeping in the same room with me. She makes me lie down, kisses me on the forehead and cheek, and whispers for me to go to sleep. When she goes back to their room, she closes the door.

·

"I fit in one hand when I was born. I was two pounds," my mother tells me, smiling as she cups her hand, palm facing up. "I wasn't expected to live."

My mother seems proud of this, as if it helps define her.

I imagine Nanny carrying her around in her hand, waiting for her to die. I imagine Nanny waking up every day and looking at her, expecting her to be dead but finding that she is still alive.

·

All night nurses disrupt my medicated sleep, muttering purposefully or laughing in whispers outside my room. Their footsteps recede down the hallway, booming softly like footsteps in a cathedral.

·

The early morning sun lights the white and metallic surfaces in the hospital room. I have to squint. The curtain between my bed and the next hangs open and a woman who must be in her late twenties peers at me. She's heavy-set, with long, dirty-blonde hair and a bad complexion. When I was brought to this room late yesterday after-noon that bed was empty.

"I'm Mary," she says.

"I'm Regina."

"How old are you?" she asks.

"Seventeen," I say, but remember that I just had a birthday. "Eighteen."

She is about to say something more when a man with a thin face and wire-frame glasses holding a clipboard comes in and pulls the curtain closed. He introduces him-self as the psychologist assigned to me, explaining that he will come to see me every morning. I smooth my hair, sit up straight, and pull the covers over my lap. He sits on a chair at my bedside and looks at handwritten notes, prob-ably the things the doctor in the emergency room wrote yesterday when I'd come, unable to stop crying. I wonder what's written there. I can't clearly remember everything I said. The doctor looks up, studies my face with a cool expression. I pull the covers higher on my lap.

"You said that ghosts have been coming to you." The tip of his pencil touches the clipboard.

I nod.

"You *see* them?"

"Yes, sometimes."

He focuses on me.

"Sometimes I feel something there, and I won't look."

He fiddles with his pencil, then smiles slightly. "You know, fear sometimes creates what at first was only imagined."

I can hear Mary sighing and shifting behind the curtain. She sounds agitated.

I look down at my hands and study the edge of the sheet, lit brightly by the sun.

"How often do you see ghosts?"

I think about my father's ghost coming to me the day before. He stood near where the doctor is now.

I shake my head.

"The real reason I'm here is because I couldn't stop crying."

"Why couldn't you stop?"

Before I answer, he says, "I was told that both of your parents committed suicide."

A storm of particles swirls in a shaft of sunlight that touches the shoulder of his white jacket.

He looks at his notes again. "Did they die together?"

I shake my head no.

"I'm sorry, these notes are disorganized. I see it was five months apart."

I don't respond.

"Who died first?" he asks.

"I don't know," I say and want to laugh because I really and truly don't know and that is an odd pleasure. I do know that if I concentrate, I will remember—and I like not knowing.

•

A window fan hums in the kitchen in the big house on Park Hill in Yonkers, New York, blowing and stirring the humid summer air. My parents stand close to each other at the counter, laughing softly as they fix breakfast. I sit on Nanny's lap, facing her, her nose and forehead glistening. She lets me rub the powder puff from her compact over her cheek, frail, fine hairs beginning to show like peach-colored fur.

I like it when Nanny visits, making the trek from her small apartment a few minutes' drive away. In the warm weather, Nanny's loose skin grows hot when I hug her. She smells like talcum powder and a waxy, flowery fragrance. The red lipstick she wears gets into the tiny wrinkles above her upper lip when she sweats.

While my father cooks bacon, my mother butters slices of toast behind us. Nanny asks my mother, "He *still* has the other job?" It is my father she means, but she talks to my mother. "How can you afford this house?"

My mother looks at my father and rolls her eyes. He holds back a laugh.

Nanny fans herself with a folded piece of newspaper. "What happened to this big job he's so sure he has?"

"He's definitely getting it, Mom. They just haven't made the change yet."

"Don't worry, Mrs. Tully," my father says cheerfully, taking a step toward her, smiling. Nanny won't look at him so he turns to my mother, who gives him a quick kiss.

I cup my hand around Nanny's ear and ask her to tell me again, something she'd told me only days before.

She whispers back, "I love you best! You're *my* girl."

•

My parents throw a party in the big house on Park Hill in Yonkers. Grown-ups gather in the living room and there is a lot of talk and laughter, a record playing low in the background, Rosemary Clooney singing about the mambo.

My brother and I are the only children at the party. I am four and Jerry is five. My baby sister, Tracy, is still too small to be out of the playpen.

"Look, Mommy!" I say and dance side to side to the mambo song. The ladies laugh and clap.

Cigarette smoke drifts overhead toward the kitchen, blown by two fans set in open windows. Everyone is sweating. Two ladies take turns leaning their faces and bare necks close to one of the fans.

"Cheers, Vincent!" a man with rolled-up sleeves says to my father, who is holding a bottle and pouring more into their glasses. "And where is your mother-in-law this evening?"

"That great doorfull of a woman?" my father asks, and the man laughs boisterously. "Be glad she isn't here, Emmet, she's got a tongue that could clip a hedge."

Someone takes the needle off the record and asks my father to sing "Nell Flaherty's Drake." My father stands:

> *He could fly like a swallow or swim like a hake*
> *Till some dirty savage, to grease his white*
> *cabbage*
> *Most wantonly murdered me beautiful drake!*

Everyone smiles and claps.

"To grease his white cabbage . . ." my mother echoes, then bows her head and laughs, her eyes wet.

"Sing the part about the pig!" Jerry cries out.

> *May his spade never dig, may his sow never pig*
> *May each hair in his wig be well thrashed with a*
> *flail!*

People raise their glasses. My mother says my father's name: "Vincent," and it sounds like the noise dimes and pennies make when he jingles them in his pocket.

"My uncle Michael never sang that one," my mother announces to everyone, "and he knew them all. He and my father were *off the boat*!"

My father, who is standing in front of the screen door, takes his handkerchief from his pocket and wipes the dampness from his forehead. "Romantic Ireland is dead and gone," he says. "It's with O'Leary in the grave."

Thunder sounds just then and everyone cheers. Behind my father there is a sudden downpour.

"Ye brought the rain, Vincent!" Emmet says.

I go to my father and stand at his leg. I touch his freckled forearm and he puts a big hand gently on my shoulder, nods slightly at me.

"Thank God!" cries one of the ladies who had been standing near the window fans. "This should cool things off."

•

My father carries me along the wet sand on Far Rockaway Beach. We have been collecting shells. The tide comes in with an unexpected power, flooding him to the knees. He holds steady and we laugh. Gulls screech and wheel above us.

•

My father is at work. Nanny sits with my mother in the kitchen. They bow their heads, holding their rosaries as they recite together: "Mother of the Church, Mother of Divine Grace, Mother Inviolate, Mother Most Merciful, Mirror of Justice, Seat of Wisdom, Mystical Rose, Tower of Ivory, House of Gold, Morning Star, Health of the Sick, Refuge of Sinners, Comforter of the Afflicted, Queen of Prophets, Queen of Martyrs, Queen of Families, Queen of Peace, pray for us."

•

The doctor peers at me over his clipboard. I don't want to answer any more of his questions. I want to tell him that I'm tired.

"Do you recognize the ghosts you see?"

I feel protective of my father's ghost. I don't mention it.

In my uncle's house a few nights before I came to the ward, I woke up and there was a lit figure standing at the foot of the bed. It was leaning forward looking at me. I tell the doctor this.

"Do you know who it was?"

"No, but it was gentle. It wasn't going to hurt me."

"Was it a man or a woman?"

"It didn't seem to have a gender."

"And the face?"

"It could have been anyone."

"What do you mean?"

"All this light was coming from it. I knew if I focused on it, it might change." I pause. "It wanted to tell me something."

"It didn't?"

"I yelled, 'No!' when I saw it and it rushed away through the closet door."

He writes. "So all of this is really upsetting you."

"There are other things." I try to think of how to articulate what I want to say. "Sometimes I can't trust the laws of physics."

He waits for me to explain.

I describe how things around me distort, rooms and hallways become foreshortened, walls and floors warp. Objects enlarge and shimmer. I cannot trust a chair not to move, or a door not to open or shut of its own accord. There are sudden shocks of sound, the air vibrates. I hear breathing close at my ear, a loud staccato buzz near the back of my head, like a chainsaw. Sometimes a bitter metal smell, the taste of a nickel.

"I won't dare turn and look when those sounds or smells are behind me. I know whatever is there is awful."

He writes.

"They're horrific, these things." Not like the figure at the foot of my bed. Not like the strange, gentle ghost of my father.

"What do these *things* want?"

I struggle to answer, and then say, "To terrify me."

•

I am still a child when I find out that neither of my parents has actually ever been to Ireland and I wonder how they can love and miss a place their ancestors left before they were born. Yet somehow I understand. And even though I am young, the idea of Ireland fills me with an inexplicable nostalgia, as if it belonged to me once and I somehow lost it.

•

I sit in Nanny's lap and turn a page in *A Child's Garden of Verses*. I show her an illustration of a little girl gazing into the flames in a fireplace and seeing a castle perfectly formed there.

"The girl is imagining that castle," she says.

"Yes," I say, nodding my head. "But you can see it and so can I."

"She's *imagining* it, Reggie."

"I know, but it *is* there."

•

I wake up crying. In my dream, my mother and father drove away and left me standing outside a store. We must be in Yonkers because I am very small.

My mother comes in and holds me. I tell her the dream.

"We'd never do that," she says. "Never." She carries me into her and my father's bed. "Never never never!" she says and kisses my forehead.

I sleep with my face next to hers on the pillow.

•

Alone in the bedroom I share with Tracy, I wear a pillowcase as a veil. I stand before the mirror with my hands pressed palm to palm as if in prayer.

"Behold," I whisper, "the handmaid of the Lord."

•

In my favorite picture from the illustrated book of saints, a nun, Saint Thérèse of Lisieux, lies in a small white bed, lifting her head slightly from the pillow, a delicate ribbon of blood dripping from one corner of her mouth. I am studying this picture and Sister Maria del Rey—herself young and pretty—comes to my desk and bends close. "Saint Thérèse had a disease called consumption," she says with a gentle smile.

Consumption—the word makes me shiver.

Still smiling, Sister touches my forearm reassuringly. "Suffering brings us closer to God."

•

The doctor asks me to give him a recent example of what happened when I couldn't trust the laws of physics.

"On the desk in my room in my uncle's house . . . something moved that shouldn't have."

"What moved?"

"My hairbrush," I say with embarrassment.

I hear Mary grunt impatiently. Maybe she doesn't like listening to all of this. Or maybe there is no one really back there.

•

A nurse arrives with my first pill and when she leaves Mary pulls the curtain partly aside and asks, "Do you mind? You've got the window and I'd like a little morning light."

"Sure," I say.

After a pause she says, "It's for psychosis, in case you didn't know."

"What?"

"Thorazine. What he's starting you on."

·

I take the Thorazine, and in spite of the brightness of the morning I cannot keep my eyes open. My father comes to me in a dream, relieved when he sees me. He asks me to help him, to tell him where to go. He seems certain that I will know, but I don't, and that devastates him.

·

On Far Rockaway Beach my father and I walk where the sand is wet, the tide rushing as it comes in.

"That way," he says and points to the horizon over the sea where nothing but sky and water are visible, "between here and Ireland, is a place called Tír na nÓg."

"What is *teernanog*?" I ask.

"It's the land where there is no pain or sorrow."

I think of the old wrinkled photograph, white and pale brown, of my mother's father and his brother, my mother's uncle Michael, when they were young men, standing on rocks near the ocean. The picture, I was told, was taken on the edge of the Atlantic, just off Ireland. Maybe they had been standing on Tír na nÓg.

"Where?" I plead. I squint my eyes, searching for those rocks, but see only water.

He kneels down in the sand and points, and closely following the direction of his finger, I search the moving water far in the distance.

I don't want to tell him that I don't see Tír na nÓg.

•

Group therapy is mandatory, at six every night in a big room at the end of the hall. I join a circle of women and a few silent men. Most everyone wears bathrobes and slippers; many look startled by the brightness of the light. Almost no one's hair is combed. Some wear regulation hospital bathrobes like the one I wear, white with small blue triangles, and paper slippers. Some have their own robes and slippers from home. Still groggy from Thorazine, I stare at the robe of a woman sitting across the circle: a satin kimono printed with Japanese geishas, cherry blossoms afloat in the blue around them.

She does not look up but sits with her hands folded on her lap and hidden in the drapes of the sleeves. She is a plain, dark-haired woman in her late thirties or early forties. I can tell that she is different from everyone else here. Some sit hunched and open-mouthed, their chests caved in, while others radiate an angry energy, as if they're on the edge of something, waiting to be pushed off. The woman in the kimono is self-contained, thoughtful. There is a steadiness to her.

Though an orderly checks in every few minutes, the meeting is moderated by patients. One woman speaks the most.

My roommate, Mary, leans close to me. "That's Patricia, the permanent fixture," she says in a drowsy voice. "When I was here more than a year ago, she was here then, too."

"Hello, Mildred," a meek man in the back says as an old woman slides noisily in on paper slippers. She ignores him and sits in a chair outside of the circle and close to the door. Whenever someone speaks she crumples a piece of cellophane. A few people roll their eyes and smile, but no one gets angry.

When a thin young man speaks in a halting voice about how sad he feels, Mildred coughs, then grabs a small plastic wastebasket near her chair, hacks, and spits loudly into it.

•

The lights are low and the curtain is closed between my bed and Mary's. I hear the wheels on the medication cart as it goes from room to room. I'm very tired and wonder if I'll fall asleep before the nurse comes with my Thorazine.

"My parents," I say to myself. I like saying *parents*, making them one being instead of two.

On the verge of sleep, I feel a pleasant sensation of relief as if what happened in my family was fate. As if it was all meant to be and my parents have found each other and everything is finished. Peaceful and settled.

I hear the squeak of the wheels as the cart rolls into the room.

•

The doctor comes to see me on my second morning in the ward. I sit up on the bed, disheveled, and glance at my brush on the nightstand, thinking I should run it through my hair, but the memory of it moving across the desk feels too fresh. I don't want to touch it. I leave my hair a mess.

"I had a dream."

"What was it?" he asks, settling into the chair.

I tell him that it had to do with an old movie, *The Uninvited*, about a house haunted by a mother who had committed suicide, and how her disembodied voice filled the rooms as she cried for her daughter.

"I wondered what the ghost wanted," I say.

"You mean the one that stood at the foot of the bed in your uncle's house?"

I quake a little. "No."

"What did the ghost in the movie want?" he asks.

"I don't know. I never watched the whole movie, but I think that ghost felt guilty."

"Do you think that maybe the ghost you saw was your mother coming back because she feels guilty?"

"No, I don't think that it was my mother, and if my mother feels guilt it wouldn't be toward me."

"Why not?"

"I caused a lot of trouble."

"What kind of trouble?"

I shake my head. "I was drinking a lot and cutting class." I explain that my mother blamed it on the friends I had and arranged things so that instead of going for my senior year, I took two college classes in the summer when I was sixteen and earned my high school diploma. I don't tell him that I drank and cut class in college too.

I sit in silence, staring at the peaks and folds of the off-white blanket on my lap.

"What are you thinking about?"

"I don't like saying *my mother* or *my father*. I'd rather say *my parents*."

"Why?"

"When I say *my parents* it feels like they're together. Like they drifted apart and it took their suicides to find each other again."

He gives me a searching look.

"Do you understand?" I ask.

He nods.

"The ghost at the foot of my bed—maybe it was both of my parents mixed together."

A look of cool skepticism crosses his face.

Talking with the doctor exhausts me. I want him to leave, but he's settled into the chair and writes with determination.

"That ghost—" he begins, sitting forward.

"It was probably no one," I say, "just some random ghost passing through."

He stops pushing me and allows a long silence.

I am the one who speaks first. "My youngest sister woke up one morning and my mother was standing at her door holding a gun."

The doctor waits for me to go on.

"When she saw that my sister was awake, she left."

"Why do you think she was holding the gun?"

It shocks me, the insinuation in his voice, as if the answer is obvious. It's there too, in the way he's looking at me. I can tell that he thinks my mother intended to shoot my sister and then herself.

I scowl and shake my head. He takes note of my reaction by scribbling something. I tell myself he's wrong—it couldn't have been that. But I begin, almost against my will, to fathom the possibility. *Shoot Sheila then herself. Right there in Sheila's room. Right there where Tracy would have to find them both.*

I feel a surge of hatred for the doctor, but instead of strengthening me, the anger drains me. I stare down at the damp ball of Kleenex in my hands and say nothing.

•

The nurse brings me my pill. I take it and everything around me blurs. I feel like I will throw up.

•

I wake to the sound of my sisters saying my name.

I sit up in my hospital bed, looking for them in the overcast afternoon light.

•

We are visiting my parents' friends who have a first-floor apartment just outside of Yonkers, with access to a backyard. Their son ignores Jerry and me because we are too little, but their daughter, who wears a red hair band and is eight years old, tells my mother she will play with us. We follow her out into the backyard. Through the screen door of the kitchen, I can still hear my mother's and father's voices mixing with the voices of the other adults. Now and then they burst into loud, uproarious laughter.

The girl points up at the fire escapes that climb the side of the building. "They look like cages," she says. Back here it smells of damp red brick and ashes.

"If you stay up until dark and you sit out here," she says to Jerry and me, "you can see fireflies."

•

At the party on Park Hill, another man sings, but no one listens to him the way they did to my father. As soon as he finishes, my father is called on again.

While people gather around him, I follow my mother, who collects glasses, putting them on a tray. I want to help and try handing her a coffee cup, but a lady grasps my mother's wrist, leans close, and says, "Vincent should have gotten that promotion. It's a shame. He should have gotten it."

"Oh yes," my mother says and picks up an ashtray.

"I was surprised you didn't cancel the party," the lady whispers.

My mother shrugs, turns away. I try to hand her the cup again but she doesn't take it. She stares into the smoke. My stomach hurts.

She looks at my father, something dark in her face. I run over to him and stand at his leg.

"Vincent," she says, no noise of dimes or pennies. "Can you help me with something in the kitchen?"

A man is in the middle of telling a story. "I'll be with you in two shakes of a lamb's tail, Barbara," my father says, his face red with pleasure.

"No, Vincent," she says. "It needs to be now."

When my father returns to the room his eyes are glassy, but the guests don't seem to notice. They crowd him. Would he sing "Whiskey, You're the Devil," or the one about Johnny the roving blade?

But he does not sing. In a hollow voice, he recites Yeats:

We Irish, born into that ancient sect
But thrown upon this filthy modern tide
And by its formless spawning fury wrecked,
Climb to . . . our proper dark . . .

He doesn't finish the poem.

No one speaks. The rain has quieted outside, but the smell of it rushes through the metal screens and into the room.

•

In group therapy, a young woman named Lily who will be leaving the next day talks about how nervous she is. Though she's young, her short hair is surprisingly gray.

"It's safe here," she says, "with all of you."

Patricia and two other women speak in a chorus to Lily. "We'll miss you." "We think you'll be fine, though." "Yes, we think you're ready."

A gruff-speaking woman with messy red hair levels her eyes at Lily and says, "I wouldn't be in your position for all the world. You don't seem ready at all."

Lily starts to cry and Patricia comforts her, but no one addresses the woman with red hair.

Old Mildred kicks off one of her paper slippers and it shoots across the floor. A choked laugh sounds from the back of the room.

When another woman raises her hand and echoes what others have been saying, about how safe the psych ward of Hartford Hospital is, how glad they are to be here, I am too disgusted to hold back.

"I can't wait to leave this place!"

They turn their eyes on me. The woman in the kimono looks up for the first time. She catches my eyes, but I look away.

"How old are you?" Patricia asks.

"Eighteen."

"Are you from Hartford?" she asks.

"I'm from Santa Fe."

"Are there sunflowers there?" a quiet woman named Judy asks with musical inflection.

"Yes."

"I've seen pictures of sunflowers that are taller than people," the angry red-haired woman says, as if this is somehow an abomination.

Lily winces. The thought seems to distress her.

"Why are you here, dear?" Patricia asks.

I shake my head.

When someone repeats the question, Patricia says, in a gentle voice, "She doesn't want to talk about it right now."

When the conversation shifts, I focus on the woman in the kimono. I hope she will look at me again, but she is lost in her thoughts.

•

Most patients go to the small cafeteria down the hall. People yell while they eat. People often spill things. The woman in the kimono does not eat in the cafeteria. I, too, ask for my meals in my room.

•

Jerry and I are sitting on the living room floor in the big house on Park Hill among all the packed boxes, playing with his builder's set. "We're going up in the sky in an airplane!" he keeps saying.

I want the red plastic hammer, but he won't give it to me, so I am stuck with the yellow wrench, which is not as much fun.

In the kitchen, our parents are arguing. My mother says that Nanny has to come with us to New Mexico.

"For the love of God, Barbara. Your mother and I . . ."

"She's an old woman, for Christ's sake."

"I can't live in the same house with her."

"We have to take her. I'm going to have to get a job and we need her to watch the kids."

My father lets out a sigh. "For Christ's sake."

"You said you had the job. We've been spending money we don't have."

"Barbara, for the hundredth time, I'm sorry!"

There is a loud noise as if something has fallen or been thrown. Jerry imitates the noise by hitting a box hard with his red hammer. My father walks quickly past us with his head down. I climb onto the couch, look out the window, and watch him drive away.

When my mother comes in, Jerry asks her if Nanny is going with us to New Mexico and she says yes.

"Will we leave Daddy here?" I ask.

"No," she says quietly. "We would never do that. Besides, Daddy has a job out West. We're going there together. You know that, don't you, sweetie? We would never leave Daddy here."

•

The doctor arrives earlier than usual the next morning. His presence makes me irritable. I fidget with a damp Kleenex, bending and folding it over and over, turning it in different directions in my hand. I tell him I was close to my mother until I was about thirteen, but that's all I can think to say. I have never asked him anything personal, but today I ask, "Are you Catholic?"

He says he isn't.

He asks me if I am Catholic—if my family is Catholic.

"Suicide is the worst sin," I say. "That's the one that can't be forgiven."

I don't look at him. I press the Kleenex tight into a ball and throw it to the side. "So stupid," I say. "God forgives torturers and mass murderers, but he doesn't forgive . . ." I think of the word *despair*, but can't say it.

•

My mother doesn't like the idea of moving west when my
father is first offered the job as an auditor for the New
Mexico state welfare system, but she changes her mind
when she finds out that Santa Fe is a place where art-
ists live and work. My mother says that she has no talent
herself, but she loves *the arts*. She had wanted to study
art history in college, but it wasn't practical, so she went
to secretarial school. She says in Santa Fe there might
be some kind of administrative job she can do involving
the arts. Before we leave New York, she sits me down
and tells me all about Santa Fe. "There's a road called
Camino del Monte Sol where painters live. And a street
called Canyon Road where all the art galleries are. And
there's a famous flamenco dancer who teaches classes for
little girls." She shows Tracy and me pictures of flamenco
dancers. "They're very proud," she says breathlessly. "And
they wear heels and stomp like horses."

I contort myself into the extreme, arched posture of
the dancers. Heart racing, I watch my mother's eyes as I
throw my head back and stomp my feet.

•

My father and I bid farewell to the ocean on Far Rockaway
Beach.

"Are we going to fly that way to New Mexico?" I ask,
pointing toward the horizon.

"No. We're going that way, to the west," he says and points in the opposite direction back toward the boardwalk and the place where our car is parked. He crosses his arms and looks a long time at the sea. "There's no ocean where we're going, Reggie."

My father picks me up and carries me back to where my mother and siblings have started eating their lunch under the big beach umbrella.

I look over my father's shoulder toward the sea, searching the horizon for Tír na nÓg.

•

Facing each other, holding each other's hands, Mom and I sway and dance, singing along with the Irish Rovers:

Her eyes they shone like diamonds,
You'd think she was queen of the land,

And her hair hung over her shoulders,

Tied up with a black velvet band.

•

I throw another wet Kleenex to the side. I won't look at the doctor, but he is waiting for me to speak.

"I came East to be near my sisters, but I've only gotten to see them once."

I explain that after our mother's death, our maternal uncles came to New Mexico, and my uncle Bob from the Bronx took my sisters, who are sixteen and thirteen, back to live with him and my aunt. I didn't want to be far away from them, but there wasn't room for me so I came to Connecticut to live with my other uncle, Jack, his wife, my aunt Pat, and their two kids. I tell him how I tried a lot of times to organize things so I could go visit my sisters, but it kept getting put off. Finally they agreed to Thanksgiving, but I was allowed to stay for only one day and one night.

"Do you know why?" the doctor asks.

"I'm sure it's because of Aunt Peggy. She's nervous. She made way too much food and kept chattering, but never once looked me in the eye."

I think of the fun I had with my sisters, staying up late, joking and laughing. Tracy talked about her chemistry teacher, Father Slattery with only one hand. She told us that she was going to write a story dedicated to him, called "The Hand That Wasn't There." The three of us laughed so hard our sides cramped.

I tell the doctor how tiny, airless, and gray the apartment in the Bronx is and that it makes no sense that Uncle Bob and Aunt Peggy took my sisters, who should have been living in Connecticut with the uncle and aunt I live with. The house is big and there's lots of room. It's a more stable environment. I tell him that Uncle Bob is nice, but that he has terrible dreams and yells in his sleep.

•

The doctor is asking me a question about the months between my father's death and my mother's, but I cannot concentrate enough to answer it. I am remembering the train from the Bronx back to Connecticut. It passed blackened industrial chimneys issuing smoke into the overcast afternoon. Abandoned skeletal warehouses loomed, hundreds of windows opaque with filth, many of them broken.

The train took a sudden circuitous path and I was confronted with a glimpse of ocean. Very faintly, through the walls of the train, I felt the water resounding.

•

Lying in my hospital bed, I close my eyes, resting my head on my arm, and think about bodies of water: the River Styx, the River Lethe. I think of a book I read about druids. Pagan stories of an afterlife say nothing about punishment. The souls of the dead cross a river at night. There was an etching of figures gathered at a shore. My parents are there together, I tell myself, in the shadows, breathing the ether of that other place. This comforts me. And there I am in the green velvet dress with flowers in my hair, coming out of the woods near the shoreline, watching their souls prepare to cross the water.

•

Mary slides the curtain open between our beds as I dial the phone on the nightstand. She wants to know who I keep trying to call.

I tell her that I have a friend in Hartford named Max, and explain that after I came East to live with my uncle and his family two months ago, I started taking a writing class twice a week. "That's where we met."

She wants me to describe him.

"He's tall and has very black hair. We had coffee together after each class and talked intensely about things."

"About what?" Mary asks.

"Mostly about religion, the hypocrisy of it. He told me about growing up in a family of observant Greek Jews, and I told him about growing up Catholic. We talked about the difference between being agnostic and atheist, trying to decide which one we each were."

Mary's mouth is tight and she narrows her eyes. I worry that maybe she's religious and I've offended her. "You better stop dialing the phone so much or they'll unplug it and take it. A lot of patients aren't even allowed to have a phone in their room."

"All right." There's a silence.

"Are you in love with him?" she asks, a note of aggression in her voice.

"No," I reply cautiously.

"I think you are," she says and closes the curtain in a noisy rush.

I sit on the bed and refrain from dialing the number again. Once, while Max was making a point about something, he leaned across the table and put his hand on my forearm. He smiled at me and my pulse began to toll and my breathing grew uneven.

I told him then about my sisters living in the Bronx and he said he wanted to drive me to see them. Moved, I told him that both of my parents committed suicide.

"You're the first person I've told since I left New Mexico."

After this he stopped touching my forearm when he talked. The next time after class he invited another student to join us for coffee. I tried to be casual and take part in the conversation, but I ached to be alone with Max. I felt myself sinking.

•

I left a message yesterday with Max's roommate, saying I'm in the hospital—asking him to please call. I lie on my side and stare at the phone, waiting for its urgent ring to break the silence.

•

We are in a new station wagon, on the road from Albuquerque to Santa Fe; my father is driving and my mother is holding Sheila in the front. In the back, Nanny sits behind my father. Jerry, Tracy, and I crowd together in the two seats to her right.

Nanny is quiet, and the sun through the windows makes the drifting smoke from her Salem look white and soft. On the radio, a man sings, and Jerry and I echo, "And I think to myself, what a wonderful world . . ."

My mother turns and, over the noise of the radio, says to my grandmother, "You can't tell right now, Mom, but we are actually going up to a much higher elevation. In a sense we'll be living in the mountains. Santa Fe has four very distinctive seasons. It always snows in the winter and can get very cold. The downtown area is filled with huge old cottonwood trees and there are woods if you drive up a little into the mountains, with giant aspens and pine trees."

Nanny does not respond. The New Mexico sunlight is a shock. There are no buildings like there were in New York, no two- or three-story houses, few trees and no shade. Dad points out what's written on the yellow-and-red license plates on every car that passes: *New Mexico, Land of Enchantment.*

With renewed interest, I peer out the window at the passing desert, a haze of heat and dust.

"Do you hear that, Mom?" my mother asks. "New Mexico is called 'The Land of Enchantment'!"

Nanny breathes hard out her nose.

Sheila, who has been fussy, starts to cry and Mom says we all need to get out of the car for a little while.

My father drives off the highway and up a high, narrow dirt path, tires crunching over stones, the car rocking back and forth until we reach the top. Hot, dusty air rushes us as we step onto a plateau. The amount of distance on all sides scares me. The silence is enormous.

"Look, Dad!" Jerry says. He's found a rock with a spiral formation on it.

"It's a fossil," Dad says. "A sea creature. There was once an ocean here." He shows it to my mother, who shakes her head and smiles in amazement.

Maybe this has something to do with enchantment.

Nanny, who has stayed in the car with the doors open, screams, "Ba'bra!" but my mother ignores her and my father wanders to the edge of the plateau and looks down onto the highway we were just on and past that to the mountains far off on the other side of that massive stretch of desert. "Ba'bra!" Nanny screams again. "Ba'bra, for God's sake!"

I follow my father, but stay a few feet back from the edge. He squeezes his filterless Pall Mall between his fingers, draws hard at it, and throws the burning stub onto the ground. He lifts his head and exhales. The smoke disappears in a wind that stirs dry dirt off the brown land.

Sheila, in my mother's arms, keeps grabbing the little white hat off her head and throwing it, and Tracy keeps retrieving it.

"Ba'bra!" Nanny continues to scream from the car.

My mother's refusal to answer makes me laugh, although I know it is not really funny. Far across the highway, tall cliffs blaze red in the afternoon sun, deep shadows filling the crevices. The hair around my face is damp with sweat.

Now and then, as my grandmother calls out to her, I hear my mother snicker. My father points into the distance, showing us two ranges of mountains to the north: the Jemez and the Sangre de Cristos.

I think of inviting Nanny to come see the mountains and the view, but I don't—I can't imagine her standing on the dust and rocks.

In the car, parked at an angle on the uneven dirt path, Nanny's lopsided shadow leans and shifts. The giddy feeling that comes with ignoring her unsettles me. I run to the car and climb in to hug her. I'm surprised when she returns my embrace, holding her cigarette aloft, and—for a little while—she is quiet.

•

The morning of my First Holy Communion, the massive doors open and, single file, we leave the fragrant darkness of Saint Francis Cathedral, my first grade classmates and I, all dressed like little brides and grooms.

Outside the wind is cold and the New Mexico sunlight hurts my eyes.

When we get home, Mom takes my hand. She leads me to her room and closes the door. She smiles and helps me take out the bobby pins that hold the veil to my head. When it's off, she raises the veil and for a few quiet moments we study the delicate floral intricacies of the lace. She lays the veil carefully in a big, flat box between two crackling sheets of crepe paper.

•

In the hospital I begin to write in a journal. I try to describe what is happening to me, to name the states when I cannot trust the laws of physics.

The word *enchantment* keeps coming to me. I write it down. I think of fairy tales I read when I was little. Under the dominion of an occult force a girl becomes a withered old woman. Or her feet root themselves into the ground so she cannot leave the yard around her parents' house. The world goes crooked. Objects become sentient. The air rings with disembodied voices.

I write: *I am subject to enchantments.*

•

Mary, who has been given an injection of some kind, asks if I will pull the curtain open. I find her against a bank of pillows with the sheet covering her to the waist, her head weighted so heavily back on the pillows that her throat looks arched. She asks in a slow voice, sad and childlike, "Where's the sun?"

"It went behind the clouds," I say.

•

While Mary is sleeping, I dial Max again as quietly as I can and let it ring for a long time. There is no answer.

•

Uncle Jack drops by briefly with some of my things. He tells me that Tracy and Sheila know I'm in the hospital. We telephone Uncle Bob's apartment and I talk to them.

"I'm fine," I say. "I just started crying and couldn't stop. I'm not going to stay in here long."

I hear hesitation in their voices, but I get them to talk about other things, kids in their schools they've made friends with. Sheila says she's going on a field trip to New York City with her class.

Uncle Jack mentions that Jerry, who is back in Santa Fe living in our parents' house and cleaning it out, doesn't know I'm here. "We don't need to call him, do we, Reg?"

"No," I say. "No reason."

•

Dad has bought Mom a new camera. It is small and held to the eye, not to the chest or stomach like Dad's Brownie box camera. Mom's eye and the camera's must be in synch. It sees what she sees.

I watch her on the lawn, watering the trees. After she turns off the hose, she crosses the street and holds the camera to her eye. She does this a few times, and then backs up a little farther.

Later, she comes in, removes the film, and drives away to drop it off for developing. I get the camera and take it outside, cross the street, and stand where she had been standing.

Is it the height of the trees she's charting? When we first came to this house, the ground was unplowed, unirrigated desert land, dry and hard. My mother worked it until it was rich and black, the hose and sprinklers on for long hours every day until water ran over the sidewalks and down the sloping street. She planted gardens and a lush lawn, a willow tree and poplars that have grown into giants. In the dry desert neighborhood, our house is enclosed in its own forest of shifting shadows.

·

One summer afternoon, we are zooming home on the highway, sweaty and mosquito-bitten after a visit to the river in Villanueva. Mom turns the radio up when a song we love by Ed Ames comes on. Dad knows the verses and starts singing, and we join in with the chorus, loud and in unison, imitating the deep-throated sincerity of the singer:

> *Muh-rye-ahhhhh!*
> *Muh-rye-ahhhhh!*
> *They . . . call . . . the . . . wind . . . Muh-rye-ahhhhh!*

•

I am in the backyard dancing. Mom is hiding behind the curtain, watching me through the window of her room. I pretend that I don't know she's there.

•

The phone rings and I jump, heart pounding. I try to calm my breathing. Mary opens the curtain just as I lift the receiver.

"Hello?" My voice trembles.

"Who is this?" a woman asks. "Where's Mary?"

•

Nanny does not like our house in New Mexico. It is in a development on desert land just off the highway to Albuquerque. New houses are being built around it; construction workers yell at each other in Spanish between the deafening sputter of a power saw.

I like visiting Nanny in her room, where she sits on a chair most of the time with her door ajar, smoking Salems. She gives me Mounds bars and Hershey's Kisses, sings to me, "I love you, a bushel and a peck! A bushel and a peck and a hug around the neck." She calls me sweetie and tells me what a good girl I am. She praises my drawings and tapes them to the wall under her crucifix. I can close my eyes when I hug Nanny and feel the hard drum of her heart against my arm, and traces of my mother are there.

•

Dad takes Jerry and me to church. Mom stays home with my sisters and Nanny. I stare up into the colored glass windows as the priest talks in a droning monotone. He captures my attention when he utters the phrase "banished to the desert." "Banished" sounds just like "punished." "Punished to the desert," I whisper to myself.

After church Dad drives along a dry stretch of mesa and pulls into a gas station. While the car is being filled he digs two dimes out of his pocket and goes in and buys Jerry and me each a Coke. We wait in the car with our Cokes while he talks to the attendant, who points up a dirt road.

The car climbs up the bumpy earth and stops at a square adobe building where five or six cars are parked. There are no windows, just a big sign with a black-and-white cartoon bear I recognize from a television commercial. The bear is going down a river on a boat, holding a bottle of Hamm's beer.

Dad tells us to stay inside the car, and we kneel on the seat, looking out the back window, watching a cloud shaped like a spider slowly break apart, the legs moving off in different directions.

When Dad comes out later, he squints and shields his eyes from the sun. He slams the door and fumbles with the key in the ignition. His face is flushed and his eyes are damp. Jerry asks if we can stop and get another Coke but Dad doesn't answer, as if he hasn't heard him.

"Daddy!" I say. "Does *banished* mean *punished*?"

"Yes," he replies.

When we get home, Dad walks up to my mother and smiles as he touches her arm. He weaves slightly on his feet. Looking at his face, she recoils, turns back to the dishes. I sense that there is something different about my father, but I don't understand why my mother doesn't like it.

He goes to the living room, but my grandmother gives him a warning look. He turns and heads out into the backyard, where he stands for a while, then settles into a patio chair, crossing his legs. I press my face against the mesh of the screen door and watch him as he stares at the ground.

•

Hours go by slowly in the hospital.

I keep thinking of the gentle figure at the foot of my bed in my uncle's house. When I close my eyes I can see it. Though the face is generic, unidentifiable, the eyes are full of shock and a nervous desire.

•

In the high school library in Santa Fe, I look at a big volume about alchemy. I turn the pages and come to a series of etchings that depict the alchemical process. In the first, a man and woman get into a bath naked. In the second, they have intercourse in the water. In the third, they die together in that same water, arms around each other. My eyes dart through the text on the page: *marriage and death; union is a manifestation of the mystery; they dissolve and lose their discriminating state.*

•

Mom wants to watch a romantic movie on television.

"You kids won't like this," she says, smiling as the credits roll over cityscapes of Paris. The others go to their rooms or to do other things, but I remind her that I'm eleven, almost twelve, and I want to see it with her.

"All right, sweetie," she says and smiles at me.

The dark-haired elegant woman in the movie has large ironic eyes and a small, ever-present coy smile. The tall handsome man in a suit seems to follow her lead moment to moment. They end up in her hotel room.

"I'll sleep on the balcony," he says to her.

"You could, you should, and you shall," she replies in an enigmatic French accent.

"I love this!" I say.

Mom laughs. "You're saying that to please me, sweetheart."

"I *do* like it, though," I say and we smile at each other.

The man in the movie stands on the balcony, lights a cigarette, and looks out over the lights of Paris glistening on the Seine.

•

The curtain is open. I am attempting to write in the journal.

"How tall is Max?" Mary asks.

"He's really tall," I say. "Six two, maybe six three."

She's quiet a few moments. "And his hair is black?"

"Yes."

"What color are his eyes?"

"Brown."

She nods. "I hope he calls you."

Her tone heartens me. I want to tell her that he loves Bob Dylan, that he sang me a verse from "Sad Eyed Lady of the Lowlands," and that he knows all the words to every song on *Highway 61 Revisited*.

I turn back to my journal and write:

> *My warehouse eyes, my Arabian drums*
> *Should I put them by your gate*
> *Or, sad-eyed lady, should I wait?*

•

It's a Saturday afternoon and we leave Nanny at home and drive along the Española highway, stopping at Camel Rock, a hill on a dry red stretch of desert with big slabs of rock on it that look like a camel's neck and head. We climb the hill, but the head is too high up on the neck for even Dad to climb on.

On the way home, Dad teaches us to sing "Who Threw the Overalls in Mrs. Murphy's Chowder." He sings the verses and we all sing the chorus boisterously over the noise of the wind coming in the car windows:

It's an Irish trick, it's true,
I can lick the mick who threw
The overalls in Mrs. Murphy's chowder.

The sun breaks in flashes into the car, sun-shade-sun-shade, as we pass along a tree-lined dirt road through the village of Tesuque.

Jerry wants to tell a joke. "What time is it when an elephant sits on your fence?"

"What time is it?" we all ask.

"Time to get a new fence!"

Everyone laughs, even baby Sheila.

"What is black and white and gray all over?" Mom asks, a mischievous smile on her face as she peers around at us in the backseat.

"What? What?" we all call out.

"Sister Mary Elephant."

We roar with laughter.

•

I leave my room to walk in the hospital hallways, but I'm restricted to the seventh floor. I press my forehead against the cold glass of a window and look down at dirty snow banked along the sidewalks, cars passing on the wet street.

A quiet man with a pockmarked face whom I've seen in group therapy walks by, avoiding my eyes. He stops in the middle of the hallway, hunching, standing still. When I pass him I see that he is staring, captivated, at the floor. He mouths a few words then smiles widely, a stiff, joyless smile, his entire body held in a kind of contraction.

He is communing with someone he is afraid of. Someone I can't see.

·

Nanny's window faces the backyard, which looks west. I peek in from the hallway. Nanny is sitting in her chair. The sun sets and red light leaks in through the venetian blinds, igniting the mirror, the edge of her dresser, and parts of the floor. I come in and stand near her. She squints against the red light and tries to wave it away like an insect. A slender line of red brightness hits a picture on the wall of a dove with its wings spread wide, a delicate silver halo over its head. Nanny tells me that the Holy Ghost is the most mysterious part of the Trinity because it is a dove, but also it is a beam of light and sometimes nothing but air. Still it is filled with the power of God.

I say that in our house there is also a trinity: the mother, the father, and the holy grandmother. I sit on the floor and draw her a picture: the holy grandmother first, then the holy mother and then the father, not "holy" because I know she will like it better this way.

.

"Girls. Girls, come here, I want to show you something."

Tracy, Sheila, and I follow Mom out and she squats down near some of the plants, lifts a leaf, and shows us tiny strawberries, mostly white, a faint blush of pink on their tips.

"They're babies," she says and smiles up at us.

.

In first grade, Sister Maria del Rey teaches us about molecules. She tells us that everything—the desk, the pencil, our clothes, even our skin—is composed of microscopic particles that revolve around one another on tiny orbits.

It intrigues me that all solid things are made of molecules, but I am astonished when Sister Maria del Rey says light is also composed of waves and particles. When light is switched off, what happens to the molecules?

At home, as my mother turns the flame down on the Minute Rice and puts a lid on the pot, I tell her about molecules.

"Even your breath is made of molecules," she says. "And even a smell that you can't see is made of molecules."

"Even a smell?" I ask. I pick up an orange, hold it a few inches away, and smell it. "So molecules of the smell are on the air now?"

"Yes, and some are even in your nose."

Suddenly there are no boundaries between the orange and me. Smelling the orange, I have taken on its nature. The orange, for a little while, is inside me, and when the smell is gone, the memory of it is so powerful I can conjure it again.

I marvel at how easily something so different, so separate, can invade me. How seamlessly we can take on the natures of other things.

•

For my tenth birthday Mom has bought me a professional set of oil paints and brushes and helps me arrange my easel in a corner of the living room near the piano. Having looked through her book of Degas prints for ideas, I paint a ballerina sitting backstage with one leg in the air as she ties the ribbon on her shoe.

Flecks of paint get on the piano, the wall, and the floor, and the smells of linseed and turpentine pervade the house. Mom doesn't mention these things as she comes in quietly to watch me work. Respecting my concentration, she leaves the room just as quietly.

•

In group therapy I sit across from the woman in the kimono, whose name I have learned is Bea. I find myself talking, words spilling out of me—about the ghost at the foot of my bed in my uncle's house. I say that it might have been both of my parents mixed together, or maybe neither of them. "Spirits are drawn to me because there is a door in me that's open but it shouldn't be."

There is silence. I have said all of this while looking at the floor. I think that I should stop talking but I don't. I tell them that it is important that I don't look at the spirits. It is important that I resist, that all I have is resistance. I tell them that I worry that my eyelids will get tired one night and betray me by opening. That is the hard work of getting through the night. Keeping my eyes from opening.

I tell them that if I open my eyes I am afraid I might end up staying in the ward forever. That I won't be able to leave.

I look at Bea. She gives me a tender smile.

Everyone is still silent, all looking at me, waiting for me to go on. I change the subject and talk about the theater party I attended in Santa Fe this past summer, and describe the two handsome actors who called me Lady Ophelia.

Tears come to my eyes, but I don't know why. Mildred crinkles cellophane.

"You seem like you could be a good actress. You're expressive," Patricia says.

"I *was* an actress," I say.

Mildred crinkles cellophane.

I continue, "Somehow I lost track of that."

"How can you say you *were* an actress? You're young. You can still be one."

A spark of excitement shoots through me as I talk about playing Heidi when I was nine, how I sang and acted, how I was told that I had a true gift. "My mother was very proud . . ."

Mildred crinkles cellophane again.

"Be quiet!" I yell.

A few people laugh with surprise. Mildred stops.

Bea beams at me. "You're just what this room needs," she says from across the circle.

I continue to talk about *Heidi*, about the tiny gold trophy I was given and the bouquet of half a dozen baby red roses. As I speak, I picture myself on a stage, graceful and expressive and urgent. I am performing for Bea and she sees me. But as I continue to talk, I find her looking down and I panic. *I've lost her*, I think. I keep my focus on her until she looks up. My disappointment must be evident because Bea nods apologetically and I forgive her moment of wandering.

•

Mom registers Jerry, Tracy, and me for a series of weekend theater workshops with a director named Mrs.

Hatch, who is in her fifties and wears bright kaftans. Her gray hair curls in a flip at her shoulders. We meet in an old Baptist church that has been refashioned into a theater. Before we begin, we are taken on a tour. A theater, I discover, is filled with mysteries: the hidden backstage where the actors must creep undetected during rehearsals and performances, a deeper backstage area where sets are built and props are kept, and a winding, unlit staircase that leads to the narrow balcony above.

We all sit in the first few rows of audience seats while Mrs. Hatch stands on the stage. "In our theater we do not have the luxury of elaborate costumes or scenery, but we do have artistic imagination and originality, and you will learn to posture gracefully." She turns and reaches out her arm as if greeting someone invisible.

She shows us a picture of Sarah Bernhardt, surrounded by lilies. She tells us about the fourth wall. Walking from one side of the stage to the other, holding one arm before her, she says, "This is the fourth wall, which exists between the performers on the stage and the audience. It is a wall that you cannot see but must *feel*. When we are on the stage performing for the audience, we must also behave as if they do not exist."

•

"Daddy, what should I change my name to when I become a famous actress?"

"Boom-Boom Latour," he says drily, and Mom snickers quietly in the passenger seat.

"No, come on!"

"Tondelyo Schwartzkopf," he says, again without cracking a smile.

"No! Come on!"

·

I decide to approach Bea after group therapy, and follow her to the door. Patricia stops me and tells me that she was once in Taos, New Mexico. "I bought a dress in a store called Martha's of Taos."

"I've never been to Taos," I say, a little flustered. "I don't know that store."

I try to catch up with Bea in the hall, and am almost close enough to tap her on the shoulder when I see her wrists hanging at her sides—both are thickly bandaged. I stop, stare into the white mask of one of the geishas on her back, then turn around and start walking in the other direction.

·

The soup is tepid when the nurse brings my tray. Still, I eat it and everything else: a dry, breaded chicken cutlet, peas and carrots, a roll and butter.

I lie curled up on my side in bed with a full stomach and close my eyes.

•

Mary's things are no longer in the room. It doesn't seem possible that she could have been released. I think of asking about her but don't. She isn't in group therapy that night, and neither is Bea. Bea's absence chills me and it occurs to me that she might have finished the job she started on her wrists.

Lily, the girl who was supposed to leave a few days ago, is still here.

•

Because my mother always seems happy to repeat the story, I ask her more than once about the bump on her nose and the slender scar that runs out her left nostril and stops at the edge of her upper lip. When she was ten she fell while climbing rocks and broke her nose. She needed sixteen stitches. For a long time her face was black and blue and swollen, and she didn't know what it would look like when it healed. She heard her father crying at night in the other room, "My little girl's face. My little girl's face." She always laughs a little when she talks about this. Her father never went in and comforted her, just sat alone in another room crying over her face as if it were something permanently lost, as if she would never have a face again.

•

In the book of Irish myths I check out from the Santa Fe Public Library there is a drawing of a beautiful woman with long hair wearing a white dress. She stands in a grove of apple trees, an apple cupped in one palm, holding it forward as if offering it. The caption under the drawing says: *Tír na nÓg, or the Land of Apples.*

•

Outside the classroom window, a tumbleweed blows across the rough pebbled tar of the playground.

"Through Communion you become one with Jesus Christ," Sister Maria del Rey says. "It is a kind of marriage."

The wind blows hard, the tumbleweed rising on air. A fine spray of dust and tiny rocks hit the window and Sister smiles as if there is a message in it for her.

I look at the image of Jesus on the holy card that she has given each of us, a familiar, fair-haired, bearded figure pointing impassively with two fingers to his heart, which is enflamed and encircled with thorns, cut in places and dripping blood.

He is a bridegroom. He wears this heart like a corsage on his white tunic.

•

The nurse brings me a pill and I take it. I want to ask her about Bea, but I am worried about what she will say.

Thorazine softens and confuses things.

I lie on my back and stare up at the white of the ceiling. I concentrate, trying to feel my mother watching me now. Her face is hard for me to recall, a face of only air. Today, my mother is a feeling that takes up the entire room, a weather condition. She is something I am constantly breathing, but cannot see.

•

I stir between sleep and waking, sensing Bea's presence. I think it's Bea's ghost, already an itinerant among others. Opening my eyes, I see Bea standing in the doorway, wearing pants and a dark blue coat.

"Good-bye, Regina," Bea says. "Good luck with everything."

"Good-bye," I say without energy and turn over. I stare at the window, groggy and partially numb, trying to understand what has happened.

•

I imagine that Bea has gone off to begin her new life. I promise myself that this was only a stopping point for her. A time to rest after a terrible mistake. She never belonged here and maybe neither do I. When the doctor comes I tell him I want to leave and he says I have only been here four days and should stay, at least, a few more. I tell him I don't want to be here. I don't tell him I have realized something important, that I am an actress and that everything might be all right in my life if I go to college in Santa Fe and become part of the theater department.

"I am suffering from grief," I say in a tired voice. "And I have an overactive imagination. That's all. I don't think it's good for me to be here anymore."

He seems startled but, to my surprise, agrees to let me leave. "But you have to keep taking Thorazine. If you don't take your pills, you'll end up back here."

.

On the spine of one of the books on my father's shelf glows a title engraved in gold: *The Marriage of Heaven and Hell*.

.

I draw for Nanny: a picture of Saint Thérèse all in white, lying in her sickbed. With a red pen, I make the dribble of blood at her lips. I keep adding to it, a little bit at a time, until it pours down over her chin, neck, and habit.

.

From the ward, I call Tracy and Sheila and tell them that I plan to go back to Santa Fe. They tell me that they do too, and that Uncle Bob has said that at the end of the school year he will make arrangements for them to live with the families of their friends.

.

As she pushes me down the corridor, the nurse explains that it is routine—that all patients leave the psychiatric ward, or any part of the hospital, in a wheelchair. I wear the clothes and coat I arrived in, and hold my purse on my lap. I glance into the rooms I pass. Everything is off-white: the walls, the curtains, the nightgowns, even the faces. I tell myself that I am no longer one of these half-dressed figures.

Lily steps out of her room and watches me. I wave but she tightens her mouth and frowns. I start to worry that someone's going to stop me and make me stay.

I take a few deep breaths as I wait with the nurse in front of the elevator. The doors open and she pushes me on. Lily stands, watching as the doors close.

•

From my uncle's house I call Max, who answers, and we meet in downtown Hartford. We go into a store to look at posters, and I thumb through a box of postcards, most with images of great paintings on them. I stop on a print of a young, haunted-looking woman in rustic clothes, standing in green foresty bracken, one hand touching a vine. Barely discernable among the branches stand angels wearing armor. I turn it over. *Joan of Arc.*

"Look at this," I say to Max. His fingertips inadvertently brush my hand as he takes the postcard, and I feel an electric current move over my skin.

He holds and studies it, then says, "She reminds me of you."

"She does?" I ask, leaning in for another glimpse of her face.

"She's yours," he says and purchases the card for me.

We sit in a café sipping hot coffee, looking at the postcard.

"What is that," he asks, "in the tree?"

"An angel."

"I didn't notice that earlier." He takes it and focuses on it. "Joan of Arc is hearing voices," he says lightheartedly. "You can tell by her expression."

"She wouldn't be out of place at the psych ward in the Hartford Hospital," I say.

He puts the card down, then stares past me through the window of the café. I wait a little in suspended silence, and then say his name. He looks at me again, something closed about his face. I wanted to ask him why he never came to the hospital, but a little wall has erected itself between us.

•

Waiting for the school bus at the end of the day, I stare at the mural on the wall outside the principal's office. It pictures Jesus, all lit up, having come out of the tomb. He is see-through, trees visible behind him. In a few moments, he will rise into the sky and dissipate like smoke.

•

Dad places the biggest firecracker, the star rocket, on the dark backyard lawn. "Stand away!" he says, and we all crowd against the wall near the gate.

He puts a match to it and steps away fast, instructing Jerry to turn off the porch light.

In a sudden blast of bright blue and phosphorescent green, it shrieks, shooting up into the night sky, then divides into six explosive starbursts.

"Oh, Vincent!" Mom's voice comes from behind me. "Wow!"

"Oh, Vincent!" Sheila says in a small, enraptured voice.

After an exuberant display, each starburst dwindles, breaking into blue and green particles, which, for a few moments, remain in shimmering suspension in the sky, before fading as they come back to earth.

•

On the morning after my father dies, I come home from the dorm room at the nearby college where I have been living the past three months. Tracy and I stand in the hallway hugging, both of us crying.

"Last night," Tracy says, "before Dad left for his shift at the bar, he sat in your room for more than an hour."

She tells me that Dad often sat in there, sometimes for hours, at night. I imagine her peeking her head in and seeing him, a big man with graying hair, out of place before

the yellow floral curtains and other things I left here—
bright cellophane flowers taped to the wall, a black-light
poster of a turquoise bear holding a tulip. Sometimes he'd
just sit on the bed, she says. Sometimes he read by the
light of the plastic egg-shaped lamp on the nightstand.

"But last night he sat in the dark."

I walk into my old room alone and stare. The bedspread is rumpled where he sat. I try to persuade myself
that he sat in here only because the room was vacated.
Not because he missed me. Not because there were things
he wanted to say.

A volume of Yeats lies on my nightstand. For a long
time, I am afraid to open it.

When I do, I read the words:

> *Do you not hear me calling, white deer with no*
> *horns?*
> *I have been changed to a hound with one red ear.*

I close the book. I do not touch it for days.

•

I am in the air. I look out over the clouds, the sky getting brighter the farther west the plane moves. Halfway
to New Mexico, I go into the bathroom, and pour my
pills down the toilet.

PART TWO

As I climb the three steps onto the stage, I am still not certain what moment from my life I want to re-create.

My new college acting teacher, Kim Stanley, has called on me in class. She's told me to perform a "private moment." I am supposed to imagine myself in a particular place at an emotionally powerful moment in my life when I was alone. I am to try to relive the experience by recalling the sensory environment. She's told us that it is not important to show the audience anything or to act anything out. It is about trying, through our senses, to bring the moment back. It is about the state of being, and about believing in the reality of the experience.

I stand in the middle of the stage and begin to sob. I struggle to concentrate, remembering what Kim asked us to do. I am afraid to find myself back in my childhood house, so I think about Uncle Jack's house in Connecticut and see flashes of the bedroom, late afternoon light coming in the window. I try to think of something else, but the room in Connecticut persists.

Kim's voice breaks through. "Thank you."

I lift my head.

"Come to my office after class, Regina," she says.

•

I find my sisters at the window in the living room, watching the trees lean and bend in a strong wind.

Dad has been dead three months.

"What are you guys doing?" I ask.

Tracy looks at me as if I am interrupting. She says nothing, and when I ask again, her mouth tenses and she gestures to the trees. But I know there is something more to what they are doing at the window. The same soft expression is on each of their faces. I also know that I am not part of what is between them.

Sheila glances at Tracy with wide green eyes. The wind intensifies and the trees go wild. At first I think my sisters are thrilled, but then sense they are frightened. I step back and sit down in our mom's brown chair in the gradually darkening room and watch them. I am closer to adulthood, while they are both stuck between childhood and adolescence. Studying their profiles, I see them tense at the hum of an approaching car, and then sigh when it passes. I understand now. They are waiting for Mom's white Rambler station wagon to pull into the driveway, worried that—like our father—she won't come home from work.

Except for Sheila's single word, "Wow," repeated every now and then, we are quiet, listening past the rushing of the leaves.

Before the sky has gone fully dark, we hear an engine slow and grow louder. When we hear a door slam and the jingle of keys, my sisters breathe a sigh of relief. They go out onto the porch to greet her, but I stay in the near darkness of the living room. I want to go with them, but something holds me back.

•

"The great director Harold Clurman used to tell me that I could be standing in a snowstorm and imagine myself in hundred-degree heat. I think you have the same kind of imagination," Kim says as we sit facing each other in her office.

She is heavyset with white-blonde hair streaked gray. In her long purple velvet dress, she exudes magisterial grace. Kim was a star in the fifties and sixties, and upstairs on the mezzanine walls there are pictures of her in Broadway plays.

I have a pressing desire to tell her what a relief it will be for me to inhabit a role, to disappear into it. But I struggle to find the right words, and then I say, "I want you to know both of my parents committed suicide."

She watches my eyes. "When?"

The question stumps me. I have to concentrate. "Last year."

She wants to know where I am living and I explain that I am sharing an old house downtown with some friends from high school.

There's a silence. "Did your parents die together?" she asks quietly.

"No."

"Who died first?"

Again, I have to concentrate. "My father."

"How much later did your mother die?"

"Five months later." There is little affect in my voice.

For a while now I have not been able to remember my parents' faces, and I tell her this. She looks at me and a flux of anxiety stirs in my chest.

•

I am a plump seven-year-old in white bobby socks and brown loafers, with a pixie haircut and a freckled nose. My jumpers are a little tight around the middle, but I secretly imagine myself as a combination of Jennifer Jones in *The Song of Bernadette*, a movie my mother loves, and the nun Saint Thérèse. In one picture in the illustrated book of saints,

Thérèse stands in a garden, looking at a rose, touching it lightly and smiling. Whenever I find a flower, real or plastic, I touch it the same way and smile at it as if it were a small person.

•

Mom gets a record of fast-paced Irish jigs and we dance wildly in our socks, slipping on the wooden floor, to "O'Sullivan's March" and "The Rocky Road to Dublin."

•

Soon after a family moves into the newly constructed house next door, their dog has puppies, half dachshund and half cocker spaniel. We pick one from the litter and name her Susie. She chases toys and balls and lets Jerry pull her in the back of his red wagon. She's sweet and docile with reddish-brown fur, and when we croon at her she wags her tail. When I carry her around like a baby she looks up at me with big brown eyes.

•

We four kids stand in a little group in front of the house. Dad holds the Brownie box camera at his stomach and looks down into the window at the top, where he sees us reflected. Then he snaps.

Jerry says that the camera has an eye that's just like a human eye because the lens turns what it sees upside down. Dad taught him this, he says.

Later when the camera is on the kitchen table, Jerry calls me over to look at it.

"It came from the East," he says. "It's older than me and you."

I peer down into the square window, but all I see is a faceted chamber made of thick glass.

Jerry says, "When you press the click button, the camera remembers."

"It has a memory?" I ask.

He nods.

When the Brownie box camera is left for weeks high up on the bookshelf in the living room, I wonder if it is my father's eye and memory that are in there, separated from him.

•

I am almost always in a hurry, my mind on my classes in the theater department, or a play—running lines in my head or out loud over the noise of the car radio as I drive past the Tap Room in Coronado Center, where my father bartended into the small hours of the morning, and the Institute of American Indian Arts on Cerrillos Road, where my mother worked as a secretary. These landmarks are unavoidable, in plain sight along two of Santa Fe's main roads.

New Mexico's harsh sun lights these buildings where my parents worked and died with the same intensity as it does the rest of the buildings: the 7-Eleven, the highway department, the Pizza Hut. Everything is equal in the nearly blinding brilliance, in this supernal light.

It seems wrong that these places blend in so easily. Sometimes I drive to the Tap Room or the Institute of American Indian Arts, park, and try to get things clear in my mind. I imagine my mother's white Rambler station wagon, or my father's brown Chevy sedan, parked beside my used Mustang.

I imagine my mother inside at her office desk, typing in that clean white adobe interior. Or I picture my father filling glasses with ice in the cool red dark of the Tap Room, dragging a damp cloth over the polished wood surface of the bar. The simple tasks of the living.

•

"What's wrong, Reggie?" Kim asks. She has insisted I come to her office. I could barely keep my eyes open in her class.

"I didn't sleep enough last night," I reply.

"Why not?"

I try to make something up, but I'm too tired.

"I felt something in my room."

"What do you mean?"

"Something standing near my bed."

"A nightmare? A hallucination?" she asks.

"I guess you could call it that," I say groggily and smile, trying to lighten things.

She pauses. "What did it look like?"

"I wouldn't look at it."

"How do you know then, that something was there?"

"It's like when someone's in the room with you, you know."

She waits for me to say more.

"It made quiet sounds. And sometimes I could smell it. It's hard to describe. A sour . . . burning smell."

"Darling, I want you to talk to me about what happened in your family."

She reaches across the desk and I give her my hand.

"Start at the beginning."

I want to please her but I have no idea what to say. Where is the beginning? Is there a beginning?

I close my eyes. Everything is white.

"Darling . . ."

I don't want to do this. "My mother," I say, and pause.

"What about your mother?"

"My mother . . . was unhappy." My mouth and tongue and the back of my throat are numb.

"Always?"

"No. Sometimes she'd get really upset when I was little, but then she'd be okay. Things would be fine. It was really the last three or four years she was alive that were . . . bad."

"Try to be specific," Kim says. "About the last three or four years."

"She . . . *fell apart.*" The words are flat and I don't like saying them.

"When you say that what do you mean?"

The past is safer in the blur where I keep it and I don't want to touch it with words.

I focus on her hand holding mine, each of us reaching toward the other across the cool, pale wood surface of the desk. She is fifty, but her hand is soft and plump—as graceful as a hand in a Renaissance painting. Her hand wants me to speak. But my mother and father have settled somewhere so deep in me, and anything I can think to say will only reduce them.

I shake my head.

"You said she fell apart," Kim reminds me.

The words "fell apart" conjure a cartoon reel, a clown figure with wild hair, gesticulating and jumping, then falling awkwardly down and breaking into pieces. I suppress a laugh.

Kim withdraws her hand and sits back.

"I'm sorry," I say. "I'm very tired."

·

Mom is playing the soundtrack to *Hello, Dolly!* in the living room, while Tracy and I help her fold clothes on the couch. Barbra Streisand is speaking some of the words in the song she's singing, in a voice that Mom says imitates Mae West. At one part, Mom drops a towel, puts her hand on her hip, and speaks along, doing her own Mae West imitation. "And on those cold winter nights, Horace, you can snuggle up to your cash register. It's a little lumpy, but it rings!" Tracy and I giggle along with Mom as she picks up the towel again.

•

Early in the semester, I am cast in a comedy, *The House of Blue Leaves*. I play the role of the Little Nun, and wear a habit borrowed from the Sisters of Loretto. My character has come to New York for the pope's visit. Two other nuns and I climb a fire escape for a better view over the crowds. The tenants invite us inside.

I open a kitchen cabinet. "Peanut butter!" I cry joyfully. "They have peanut butter!" I turn to the audience and say with hushed seriousness, "We're not allowed peanut butter."

A loud chorus of laughter rises from the darkness.

•

At a party at someone's second-floor apartment after the show, I stand out on the balcony talking and sipping beer with Tom, another actor from the play. He's from Michigan, tall with light brown hair and a strong physique. He says he loves the fact that I come from Santa Fe. He lives in the dorms, where everyone is from somewhere else.

There's a big crescent moon in the clear sky, and I wonder out loud if it's waxing or waning. "It's waxing," he says and explains that you can tell by the way it's facing.

"I've heard that a waxing moon is auspicious," I say and he smiles.

We leave the party together and walk downtown to the river. It's late and no one's there, the park and river lit only by the waxing moon and the lights of houses across Alameda Street.

We lie down on the grass by the rushing water and kiss.

•

A lanky Franciscan friar, Father Godfrey, comes to our fourth-grade class, wanting to know if there are any small saints among us. He wears black plastic glasses, and it's hard to see his eyes behind the Coke-bottle lenses. He asks everyone to hold up their hands so he can look for the stigmata, the mark of Christ's suffering.

A little girl with long eyelashes and very dark skin, Carmelina Bustamante, tells the story of how her uncle, wanting to feel Christ's suffering, pounded a nail through one of his feet. Father Godfrey nods his head and smiles as if he approves of what the girl's uncle did.

He draws a diagram on the chalkboard. In the top box, he lists the venial sins. Below that the mortal sins, the worse they are, the lower on the list. At the very bottom, the worst sin is the sin of *despair*, or *suicide*.

"Do you know what suicide is?" he asks.

The same girl whose uncle hammered a nail through his foot raises her hand. "When someone hangs himself."

Father Godfrey nods. "No one has the right to kill himself in any way at all, hanging or shooting or stabbing himself in the heart. Suffering is fine, good even, as long as you are not trying to die. Only God has the right to end a life. Anyone who does such a thing removes himself from the grace of God."

He circles the word *despair* again and again and puts an exclamation point next to it.

•

Every time Mom talks about finding a job, Nanny yells. Mom reminds her that that's one of the reasons Nanny came with us to New Mexico, so she could help take care of us kids, and now it's been almost two years since we've been here. Mom says she has to work, and she's not going to fight about it anymore.

"Your husband should be able to support you," Nanny says. She slams the door to her room. Hours later, I come in from playing and see that Nanny's door is still closed. I can hear her muttering. When I knock, she opens it a small bit and looks down at me.

"What's wrong, Nanny?" I ask.

She lets me in and closes the door again.

There is noise from a new construction site on the street right behind us, a chainsaw, then a man yelling a string of words in Spanish.

"Those men!" she says, and makes a face as if she smells something terrible.

I think of telling her what Jerry told me, that those men look at pictures of naked ladies in magazines. But I can't bring myself to say it.

•

My father is driving and I am in the backseat. Noticing one of his magazines on the floor, I pick it up and begin searching for bad pictures. There are only pictures of buildings and typewriters and businessmen in ties. On one of the back pages I find a very small black-and-white print of a heavyset, naked woman sitting near a river. Quietly, I tear her out and put her into my pocket so I can show Nanny. A sensation that is awful and thrilling fills me. When we get home, I go to her room, close the door, and show her the picture. "Look what I found in my father's magazine."

She peers into my eyes. "He's disgusting."

She stands up and opens her dresser drawer. She gives me a quarter and half a Mounds bar.

I want to cry. I leave her room and go into the bathroom and rip the little picture up into tiny pieces and drop them into the toilet. Some of the pieces float, but most sink to the bottom.

•

On a mild morning, Mom tells us kids that she has gotten a job as a secretary at the Institute of American Indian Arts and will be starting soon. She is nervous to tell Nanny, but she does. Nanny surprises us all by remaining calm.

•

I open my bedroom door early on the morning of my mother's first day of work and see her all dressed up, standing in the hall in her high heels, looking down at my grandmother's full bedpan, some of its contents slopped out onto the floor.

My mother gags, covering her nose and mouth with her hand. She stays there, staring like she can't quite believe it. She knocks on Nanny's door and says, "You're as healthy as a horse, Mom. You can make it to the toilet."

There is silence from behind Nanny's door.

My mother bends down and carefully lifts the bedpan, then takes it into the bathroom and closes the door.

Every morning that week, my grandmother puts out a full bedpan. I watch from a spot behind my slightly open door. I know on some primitive level that I am witnessing a mystery, something terrible and important, like the moment when the disc of bread in the priest's fingers turns into the flesh of Christ, and the bread is no longer wheat and water, but blood and skin.

I go back into my room and lie down on my side facing the wall, imagining my organs as they are depicted in the children's anatomy book at school: an orange stomach, two pink lungs, and a bright purple liver. They have come loose and are floating and pulsating inside me. I have to keep my mouth closed because if I'm not careful, they will all come up out of my mouth onto my pillow.

·

I drive to Albuquerque and visit Jerry, who has transferred to the University of New Mexico and is living in a small house with two other guys. I ring and he opens the door, music blasting on the stereo behind him.

"Hey!" he says, smiling as he greets me with a hug. He is wearing wire-frame glasses, his hair almost to his shoulders.

All the curtains in his house are closed, keeping out the daylight, and the air inside is stuffy and reeks of pot smoke. I am acquainted with both his roommates, high school friends of his from Santa Fe. Each says a groggy hello. In the haze, they appear to be sunken into a stained yellow couch with its insides spewing from one arm. Cups, a full ashtray, and fast-food wrappers cover an old coffee table.

Before the semester began, Jerry came to Santa Fe and visited me at the old house downtown on Manhattan

Avenue where I live with four friends from high school. But this is the first time I've come to his place.

He hands me a beer, then lights a joint to smoke with his roommates.

He tells me that he still has some stuff in boxes from the old house, some books and a few things he didn't have the heart to throw away. "You're welcome to look and see if there's anything you want."

"Yeah, okay," I say. "I'll look in a while."

My eyes have adjusted to the gloom and I find myself looking into a deeper shadow on the other side of the room, a chair covered with clothes and bags, a towel draped over the back. It is the old living room chair, the brown one Mom had always sat in. I see her as she was near the end of her life, sitting in this chair, smoking and staring. I try to push away the image.

I must have stopped talking, because Jerry breaks the silence. "I kept an old painting you did, Reg," he says, smoke drifting from his mouth.

"Really?"

"Yeah, it's hanging in the hall, but you can take it if you want."

I go to the hall, which is much brighter than the main room. There is only one picture hanging, and as I approach, seeing it from the side, the pale wooden frame looks familiar. When I face the picture my stomach drops. It is the watermelon slice and pitcher on a red-and-white checked tablecloth, one of my mother's paint-by-numbers. In a flash, I see my father standing near this picture, blood on his face after a fight with my mother.

Back in Jerry's living room I sit on the floor away from and with my back to my mother's chair, but I can feel the buzz of it behind me. I break into a sweat. The walls contract and the room becomes dark and close. I worry that Jerry is in danger, cohabitating with relics. I don't know how to tell him this.

"Jer, don't you want to throw everything from the old house away?"

"I use a lot of it," he says and gives me a stoned, quizzical look. "Don't you want the picture?"

"No thanks," I reply. I don't have the energy to tell him that it was Mom who painted it and not me.

•

Kim has called me into her office again.

"You said that your mother changed the last three or four years she was alive."

I nod.

"Did something happen that you can remember, something that caused the change?"

It occurs to me that Nanny's death had something to do with it, but I cannot speak. The thought of mentioning Nanny makes me numb and tired.

I shrug and shake my head.

•

At night, when I can't sleep, I drive to the southern end of town where the main road becomes the Albuquerque highway and turn into the desert neighborhood where we lived, our house occupied now by another family, other children's bicycles on the lawn. I park across the street and watch unfamiliar figures passing back and forth behind the lit kitchen window. Do they know, I wonder, that they live in a house full of ghosts? Do they feel us there?

•

Some nights, after rehearsals, I don't go back to Manhattan Avenue. Tom lures me to his dorm room, where we make love on his narrow bed until we're exhausted.

•

The summer before I go into sixth grade, Dad develops an allergy to the sun, big red blotches forming all over his face. He has to wear a cowboy hat whenever he goes outside, and suddenly the sun seems larger and closer than I remember it being the summer before.

Dad buys Jerry a matching brown cowboy hat.

Jerry hesitates. "I don't have that allergy to the sun, Dad," he says.

Dad peers at him, then turns the hat over in his hands, looking at it. He extends it toward Jerry again. "Try it," he encourages.

Jerry puts it on and Dad says it looks good but Jerry seems embarrassed.

Dad colors slightly and smiles. "I can take it back to the store," he says. But he never does. The brown hat, too small for Dad, sits on the shelf in the living room.

.

One weekend I see Dad and Jerry outside, surveying some cracks in the concrete pathway near the lawn. Jerry is wearing the brown cowboy hat, and my father is wearing his. They stand out there in the sun with their hands on their hips.

.

All of us kids are in the car with Mom as she drives on Paseo de Peralta in northwestern Santa Fe. She stops at a gas station and when she turns the key in the ignition, she looks over her shoulder at me in the backseat where I sit between my sisters, and says, "That's the soldiers' cemetery, where I want to be buried. Remember that, will you?" She points across Rosario Boulevard at a green hill lined with square white headstones. Then she laughs slightly.

"You're not going to die," I say.

"Everyone dies," she answers. "And when I do, I want a soldier's burial."

My heart thumps and when none of my siblings speak, I say, "Well, you're not a soldier!"

"That's what you think!" she says, with a roll of the eyes and a bitter ring in her voice.

•

Usually Mom gets home from her new job before the red light coming in Nanny's window gets very dark and turns purple, and when she doesn't, it is unbearable. I think of the soldiers' graveyard, and worry that she may have driven there instead of coming home. If she doesn't come home, I don't know what I will do. Sometimes I lie on Nanny's bed, imagining a little ribbon of blood at my mouth. *I'm suffering*, I think. *That makes me closer to God.* If after the purple light has given itself over to darkness she still isn't home, I will start to cry and run into the kitchen and hug Nanny, closing my eyes and searching her embrace for the part of her that is also my mother.

•

In a magazine famous for its photographs, I turn the page to a big black-and-white picture of alleys and burned-out buildings. Someone has written *God is dead* in dark letters on the wall. The world is wide and undiscovered. I worry there are black-and-white places where God has died.

•

Susie gets heavy after being spayed. When Mom tells her what a good girl she is she gets excited and does what we call her karate jump, one little hop in the air before landing on her four short legs. If Mom says it again, she blows out once fast through her nose, then gallops up the hall, nails clicking on the tiles, comes back, then sits down and pants.

"Good girl! Good girl!" we squeal at her and she jumps again, races up the hall and back, a flurry of jingling license tags and clicking toenails.

•

Tracy and Sheila both move in with the families of friends and I pick them up one Saturday. After the family's estate was settled, each of us kids received just under $4,000, and as soon as I came back to Santa Fe, I used more than half of mine to buy a used turquoise Mustang. When I start to drive, the song "Maybellene" by Chuck Berry comes on and we decide, unanimously, Maybellene is the perfect name for the car. I drive up previously unexplored streets off Siringo Road, avoiding the old house, though we are close. I wait for one of them to suggest driving past it, but to my relief neither does. It is something I do alone. To do it with them would be too hard.

"Mom's friend lives on this street," Sheila says in a tone so casual, it is as if Mom is still alive. I find myself wondering if it's true. I sense in Sheila's voice that she just has an urge or a need to mention Mom. That it almost doesn't matter what she's saying. I hope that she won't do it again.

"Mom took me to that friend's house once," she adds, and I meet her eyes in the rearview mirror, then look away.

•

Mom shows me an old pewter-and-gray photograph, a slightly heavyset man in a suit, with white hair and thick white eyebrows, holding his hat with both hands near his chest.

"My uncle Michael," Mom says, keeping her eyes fixed on him, a soft, flushed smile on her face. She has talked about Uncle Michael before, her father's brother. They immigrated to America together as young men. He was always particularly kind to her. She was his favorite.

"What a nice man he was," she says. "I miss Uncle Michael."

•

The south side of town, where Cerrillos Road becomes the Albuquerque highway, is still undeveloped, hardly any stores, just vast stretches of mesa for miles. A small adobe building sits isolated far back off a dirt roadway. Its sign is almost as big as the building and reads *The Rock Shop* in big dark letters, uneven and jagged, as if they themselves were formed of rocks.

It's Saturday and while Mom plants squash and pumpkins in the back garden, Dad drives us kids here. It's a form of heaven for Jerry. I gravitate to a huge gray stone cut open to reveal a cave of jagged purple crystals, but Jerry keeps tearing me away from it to see different fossils: flat sandstone with imprints of small fish; gray stone with images of veined leaves and more sculpted, round, beetle-like creatures with delineated rib cages, some of them as large in diameter as a baseball, but flatter.

"Trilobites!" Dad says when Jerry shows him. Jerry repeats the word twice in quick succession.

I breathe in his enthusiasm and it catches in my lungs. "Trilobites," I say, exhaling the word.

.

The whole family is in the car.

"What did the duck say when he bought lipstick?" Jerry asks us.

"What? What?" we demand.

"Put it on my bill."

.

"An actress," Kim says to me, "needs to have access to her own history. When you work on a play, you have to look at the dramatic arc. You break it down into manageable parts, into beats. See how every event leads to the next."

I nod as if I understand. But it is as though each death were an explosion that erased the connections between things. In my mind a fizzing whiteness hovers, particles refusing to settle.

Kim says I might begin by asking myself what my mother had wanted, and what my father had wanted. Why had they wanted these things? What were the obstacles that kept them from accomplishing their objectives?

•

I am in my dorm room when my father calls. "Why don't you come by the Tap Room tonight and say hello," he says.

"I'll try."

"I'll look for you."

"Okay."

Silence.

"Your mother called you very late one night and no one answered."

"Oh, sometimes I study late with friends."

Silence.

"I better go," I say.

•

Early the next morning, Jerry and Tracy knock on my dorm room door.

"What's wrong?" I ask.

They come in and sit down, Jerry on the bed, Tracy on a chair. I close the door and look at them.

"Dad's dead," Jerry says plainly.

"No. No. No." I scream, flail my arms, and start to cry. "How?"

"Car accident," Jerry answers in a monotone.

I scream and yell and pace. I am unsure what to do with myself. I look again at them, waiting to hear that it isn't true.

Jerry says, "It wasn't a car accident."

•

Only once do I look in the book *The Marriage of Heaven and Hell*. I read the phrase: *The cut worm forgives the plow*. I slap the book shut.

•

The window of my old bedroom is open and morning breezes come in through the screen, the curtains shifting. A gust of April wind rushes through the leaves of the trees, a sound I always took comfort from as a child, pretending it was the ocean crashing at a shoreline. The trees my mother planted have always been steadfast outside my window, waving in wind or standing unmoving on still, hot days. At night, they made the soft brushing sounds that led me into sleep.

I hear my sisters' voices down the hall, their words a blur but their intonations clear: quiet questions that have no answers asked to the air. I hear Mom's voice. And it is calm.

Another breeze rushes and agitates the trees. I press my face against the screen, watching them as they lean in my direction. I sense in their ache to tell me something both a plea and an accusation.

I walk down the hall. Dust motes float, glimmering in a shaft of morning sun coming in the front window. My sisters are on the couch with Mom, their laps and legs lit in sunlight, the rest of them sitting back in shadow.

Tracy, who is fifteen, wears one of my cast-off shirts, her auburn hair grown out in thick waves, wild over her shoulders and down her back.

And Sheila, at thirteen, looks eleven at the most, slender with a freckled, upturned nose. Both their faces are red and streaked with tears.

Jerry sits in a chair in a dim corner, gazing past me. His hair looks unwashed, a stubble of bright beard on his chin. He is in his freshman year at New Mexico State University in Las Cruces, a seven-hour drive south, but came home for spring break yesterday. Since earlier this morning when he and Tracy picked me up from the dorm, he hasn't said a word.

I stand in the middle of the room trying not to cry. "Mom," I say.

She seems to really look at me. She gets up, squinting as she passes through the shaft of sunlight, stirring the dust motes to a soft frenzy. She embraces me. Maybe what my father did broke a spell in her, awakened her, brought her back from somewhere she'd gone. I feel a sensation, a relief I'd always felt in her arms when I was small; the possibility of disappearing into her.

"Don't leave, Reggie," she says.

"I won't, I won't," I cry.

I hold harder to her, afraid she'll let go. On the coffee table, I see a yellow pad, things scribbled on it in pencil, some of the words scratched out: *Block's Mortuary* and the phone number. *Military Cemetery on Rosario Boulevard. Private First Class Vincent William McBride, served Korea 1952–1954.* Near the yellow pad are deep burns where cigarettes have been lit and forgotten. In the ashtray is a cigarette left to burn down all the way, a long tunnel of ash.

My mother's face feels cool and childlike as it rests against my neck.

•

Mom stands with her arms crossed, watching Nanny sleep in the green chair. "This time," she says to my father quietly, "I think she's going to die."

A little later when Mom is in the kitchen, I go in and put my arms around her. I have caught her at a good moment and she seems grateful to be approached. She puts down a spoon she is stirring something with and gives herself over to the embrace, pressing a kiss to my temple.

I want to tell her that I wish I could have taken care of her when she fit in one hand. I want to tell her that instead of having Nanny for a mother, I wish she'd had me.

•

Tracy tells me, "Dad left a note."

"What does it say?" I ask.

"It says that he loves his kids and something like, 'Barbara knows why I'm doing this.'"

·

I sit on the floor of my old bedroom, listening to my mother on the phone in her room making funeral arrangements. My father has done something irreparable. There is a new trajectory in place. Every cell and every particle around me knows how things will end. Every bright dust mote rushing through the sunlight and disappearing in shadow rings with inevitability. The house, the furniture, the trees, my brother and my sisters, even my mother—we all know, but it is not possible to accept this and keep going.

·

I am cast in another play at the college. I am Shelly, the spaced-out hippie girl in *Moonchildren*. Standing downstage, I hold a plastic bottle of bubble stuff, a delicate pink wand poised before my lips.

"Bubbles are divine!" I announce in a high-pitched voice, then blow. A flood of bright bubbles flashing prismatic colors in the spotlight floats out into the dark over the laughing audience.

·

After the play, I push through the small crowd backstage to get to Tracy and Sheila, who are waving energetically and calling out to me. When I reach them I throw my arms around them.

"You were so funny!" Tracy says.

"I loved it!" Sheila says.

I introduce them around to everyone in the show. "These are my sisters!" I say.

Everyone smiles at them. Some of the other actors hug them. It is a celebration.

"These are my sisters!" I say again and again.

•

Between classes, I go to the café in the student union building. I buy a cherry milkshake and join a table of theater students, the loudest group there, everyone speaking in foreign accents or quoting lines from plays.

A senior who has been working on Hamlet's monologue comes in and walks toward our group carrying a tattered copy of the play. Euphoric to be part of this clan, I stand up, put one hand on my heart, and with sincere regard in my voice, say, "Here comes the beauteous majesty of Denmark!"

•

Kim has grown impatient with me. The comedies I'm cast in in the department have nothing to do with her.

In those I am free, uninhibited. I have fun. But in acting class, Kim wants more from me. She wants me to get in touch with my "rage."

"How did they . . . ?"

"Guns," I say and loosely wave my finger in the direction of my head, then avert my eyes.

After an extended moment of silence, she looks through a stack of plays on her desk, finds one, and suggests that for class, I work on a scene from *The Chalk Garden*.

"You need something emotional. You have a lot to express. This girl, Laurel," she says to me about the character in the play, "is like a bomb, ready to go off."

I take the play, wondering if when Kim looks at me she sees a bomb ready to go off. I sit in the grass in front of the theater and read, frustrated that the girl she wants me to portray is only fifteen. I am almost nineteen. I want to be a young woman onstage, not a child. The character is a furious girl who steals and trespasses; a child with pyromaniac tendencies.

·

My mother and father are in the kitchen. I go in their room and look in the envelope of photographs from New York and take one out of the two of them, much younger, sitting together in an elegant restaurant with daylight coming through the windows. The forks and glasses on the table glow. My father sits on the right and my mother on the left, each delicately smiling, their hands intertwined on the table. On the wrist of her other hand, my mother wears what looks like a flower, but her hand and the flower are smudged together into a blur of molecules, something deformed-looking and mostly invisible.

The image sends a shock through me. If I show this to my father, he might explain that the camera made a mistake of some kind. But even that will not get rid of this sense of powerlessness the picture has filled me with. Something is revealed here. My mother's edges sometimes dissolve. Sometimes she is not solid, but more like a storm of air.

I take the picture and hide it under the nightstand in my room.

Dad is outside, looking under the hood of his car. Mom sits at the kitchen table with a cup of coffee, writing a grocery list on a yellow pad. I stand in the doorway and look at her hands—they are solid. I want to touch them, to make sure they feel warm at the palms and slightly cool on top. But she would see my face and want to know what's wrong.

•

For months after Dad kills himself, my sisters manage, by concentrating every night at the window, to bring our mother home from work.

Then, on the very last night of September, the white Rambler station wagon does not return.

•

My roommate, Wendy, says I got a phone call. Someone, a friend of my parents', is coming to get me.

"Why?" I demand.

Wendy is reluctant to say.

"Tell me," I insist. "It's my mother, isn't it?"

•

We are watching *Miracle on Thirty-Fourth Street*. Tracy and I sit shoulder to shoulder leaning against each other on the couch, while Sheila sits by Jerry on the floor in front of the television. The movie is about halfway over, and it is beginning to get dark outside, when Mom comes in from the kitchen and sits on the couch next to Tracy. She looks tired.

Sheila comes up off the floor and climbs onto Mom's lap and strokes her face. Submitting to the pleasure of it, Mom sighs deeply and closes her eyes. I move near her and kiss her cheek.

•

I gasp when I open the door. The large silhouette of my father looms in the shadow of the doorway. He takes an awkward step forward and becomes Mr. Murphy, my father's boss from the Tap Room, whose voice falters and hesitates: "I'll drive you . . . home."

Though the passenger seat is empty, I sit in the back.

"Where did she die?" I ask as he pulls out onto Cerrillos Road.

"At work—when everyone was gone." He pauses. "Like your father." Our eyes meet in the rearview mirror. In those three words, *like your father*, I feel him trying to reach out to me.

I hear myself ask the question, "Did she use a gun?"

His eyes find mine again in the mirror. "Yes."

I look away and watch the headlights streaking past. My tears are steady and quiet. This is not the shock my father's death was.

•

Jerry keeps a shoe box full of his favorite rocks on the floor near his bed. And there are rocks on his dresser and lining a little shelf above it. He shows me pieces of mica and flint, and pebbles he says were shaped by water, and a dry wafery rock that crumbles too easily. When talking about rocks, he has about him an air of almost breathless excitement. "This one," he says, holding a chunk of something that looks like porous cement, "is from a meteor."

I take the rock from him and examine it.

He leans forward and in a half whisper, says, "Meteors fall to earth."

Mom smiles when she comes in and sees us looking at the rocks. She has said before that Jerry has a calling, that he'll be a geologist, someone who studies rocks.

•

Jerry and I walk on the mesa with our heads down. The dry ground is riddled with stickers, stubs of cactus, piñon brush. Small grasshoppers fly out and hit my bare calves. And the occasional stinkbug runs out from under a weed. Sometimes I find broken glass, clear or bright green, or my favorite, very deep cobalt blue. I prefer the glass to the rocks, but I don't tell Jerry this, just that I like the glass, and he tells me to go ahead and put pieces of it into the bag.

"Look, Reg," Jerry says and holds up the metal cartridge of a bullet. "A gun was fired near here."

"Throw it away!" I say, but he won't. He rubs the dust off it with his shirt and places it not in the bag with everything else we found but in his pocket.

•

As Mr. Murphy turns onto our street, I ask if Tracy, Sheila, and Jerry all know. He says that they do. All the lights are on when we pull up to the house, all the windows and doors open.

I get out of the car and stand there a few moments before closing the car door. It is summer's end and the nighttime is alive. Crickets sing so loudly and with so much energy the air vibrates. Stars crowd the darkness above the poplar trees. They shake and send out wavy shimmers of light.

Tracy appears in the window of the lit kitchen. Sheila steps out of the screen door, a silhouette, her head raised, one arm gesturing in my direction.

•

I do not ask if Mom left a note, and no one mentions one.

Uncle Jack explains it will be a closed-casket wake.

Sheila starts to cry. "I want to see her."

•

"I need a new dress," I say.

"Well," Aunt Pat says, and her upper lip twitches, "what did you wear to your father's funeral? Won't that do?"

"No," I say, "it won't do."

•

With the bedroom door locked, I put on the new white lace dress, look at myself in the mirror, and remember my First Holy Communion, how, in my veil and white dress, I told my mother I was her bride, and how, at my confirmation, I took her name, Barbara.

I sit in the room in my dress and say, "Mom," to the air. Repeatedly I summon her. But nothing. Maybe she is gone. Maybe she has left no ghost, no trace. And I cannot feel my father, either. Nothing. No one. Only silence.

•

Three of the four roommates living with me on Manhattan Avenue move out, leaving only me and David, a boy I knew in high school. We don't have much furniture, just some ratty old pieces from the Salvation Army, and mattresses on the floor of each room. Tracy moves in with us. She and her friend Theresa have stopped getting along.

We don't keep regular hours. In the middle of the night, most of the lights are on. David has a good job as a waiter at the Bull Ring, an expensive steakhouse, and has bought a stereo. At all hours Jeff Beck's *Blow by Blow* plays at high volume, or Traffic's *John Barleycorn Must Die*, or *Bare Trees* by Fleetwood Mac.

I've been working on a monologue from *Saint Joan* by George Bernard Shaw and stride aggressively through the rooms crying out, "We ride to Orleans! We ride in the name of God and under the orders of holy saints Catherine and Margaret."

•

Tracy has strep throat and lies on a striped mattress. She eats nothing. All she can get down is tea. She went to a health clinic and got a shot of penicillin, but it doesn't seem to help.

•

I keep forgetting that Tracy's sick, and then I pass through her room and look down at her, surprised. For two weeks now she has lain there wearing the same purple T-shirt and jean shorts.

•

I can see myself and most of the other girls reflected in the big mirror at the front of the dance studio. All of them wear tight black tops and long skirts, while I wear a white turtleneck and a pair of black tights. I am the only girl without a skirt, and everyone but me has an identical pair of shoes, noticeably different from mine. I am also the only girl in the class with short hair. While we wait for the class to begin, the girls, all frigid-faced, stare at my reflection. I am much plumper than any of them. As the teacher turns to face the mirror, she breathes out harshly through her nose. I wonder if that snort is meant for me. Without saying a word, she begins to move, and taking my cue from the others, I imitate everything she does.

Calling one girl to the front, she speaks a flurry of Spanish words to her, then steps back and claps time as the girl, rib cage distended, head high and back, holds one skinny arm in the air, trilling her castanets to a light gallop. One foot stomps again and again as she turns. I struggle to follow the girl's lead. The teacher squeezes my upper arm as she places it in the proper position. Tears shoot into my eyes.

After the class, the teacher approaches my mother, who has been standing in the back of the studio with a group of other mothers, watching the class. She asks why I don't have the proper clothes or shoes for Flamenco. My mother apologizes, says she didn't know.

Driving home, my mother is quiet, her stare is wide as if it is taking in more than the road ahead.

"I don't want to go back," I say.

"No," she says distractedly. "Don't worry."

·

In the summer before fourth grade, I am in one of my first plays, cast in the role of Heidi. When I don't want to leave theater class after rehearsal one day, Dad laughs and tells Mom that they have a prima donna on their hands.

Dad tells me it is time to go and I respond with something he often says: "I'll be with you in two shakes of a lamb's tail."

·

I like to go to Saint Francis Cathedral downtown when no one's there and just sit and think, watching the lit votives cast moving shadows in their alcoves. It occurs to me that I should light a candle for Tracy.

Why is it so hard for me to remember that she is sick? Why am I not attending to her, trying to take care of her?

I am afraid to be a mother. It's too dangerous to be a mother. I think of the lady in the financial aid office; I've spoken to her several times on the phone and met her in person when I delivered my paperwork. She knew Mom and is very kind and encouraging to me. I wish I could call her and ask her to take care of Tracy.

•

I knock over a knickknack, a little plaster cherub head on a small blue porcelain stand. It shatters on the floor near my feet, but the face, intact, flies across the room, separate from the rest of the head, and lands under the couch. I sweep everything up but the face. Later I look under the couch, and the face lies there peering up in the darkness.

•

"Reg, will you make me some tea?" Tracy asks from the mattress.

I stand in the kitchen holding a cup under the faucet. I stare as the water runs over the edge of the cup. I can't remember why I'm here.

"Reg," Tracy says from the other room.

I pour the water in the pot. There are no tea bags.

She says it's okay.

I bring her a cup of boiling water.

•

"Your mother's suicide was a response to your father's," Kim says.

I nod.

"But why did your father kill himself?"

I want to try. I want to be able to give her answers.

Kim asks me to remember him. I think of him balancing the checkbook, the afternoon light falling across the kitchen table where he sits, the shadows of my mother's poplar trees moving on the curtain and the wall.

"Did money have a hand in things?"

I nod. "My father was supposed to get this very important job back in New York, where I was born. He was so sure he was getting it that we moved into this big house we couldn't afford."

"But he didn't get it?" she asks.

I shake my head. "We moved to New Mexico because he found a job here where he was supposed to be able to advance. But he had no luck. When I was ten or eleven, he had to take a second job at night as a bartender."

"He worked hard," she says.

I nod, but can't say more. The air in Kim's office is too full of my father: smells of metal, worn leather, car exhaust.

•

Mom says I can have the small, flat blue bottle shaped like a moon that's in the drawer with her slips and nylons.

"Your father gave me that perfume around the time he asked me to marry him."

There is only a little perfume left at the bottom, a concentrated tincture. I recoil at the dizzying fumes, like dead flowers mixed with bourbon.

"It doesn't smell nice anymore, sweetie."

Words are written on the blue, moon-shaped bottle, silvery words I can barely see: *Je Reviens*.

"It's French," Mom says. "It means 'I Shall Return to You.'"

Sometimes I see my father on a Sunday, or very early on school mornings, but he works so much, it feels like he doesn't live here anymore.

Je reviens, I imagine him saying. *I shall return to you.*

•

I am on my way to watch cartoons in the den when I see Dad sitting alone in the living room reading the newspaper. I go in, take a book from one of the shelves, and sit beside him on the couch. I've picked a book of Irish place names.

There is something almost comical-sounding about many of the names. If I were reading them to someone who wasn't Irish, I'd be embarrassed.

"Listen, Dad," I say. "Some of these names of places are funny: Abbeyfeale, Ballymoney, Clonmacnoise, Doonooney."

When I make a face, a shadow I can't quite read crosses his forehead. He nods softly with his mouth closed, then looks back at the paper. My heart pounds as if I have just made fun of Dad himself. I want to make it up to him.

"There is a river named Bride that runs through Waterford. And there is a place called Bantry Bay. And Kinsale. I really like those names. And Kinvara!"

He looks up again from the paper. "I'll tell you a funny one," he says. "Skibbereen."

We both laugh.

"It's a beautiful word, though," he says, "in its own wild way."

I find another funny one: "Castlepook!" I say and we laugh. I turn the page. "Killinaboy!" I cry out and we laugh more.

"So wild!" I exclaim, shaking my head slowly and smiling as I turn the pages. "All so wild and beautiful!"

•

Except for our hushed first-grade class entering in single file, the cathedral is empty. The dark, cold air echoes. At every turn, we are confronted by another life-sized statue. The deeper we go into the church, the worse the statues seem to be suffering—dripping blood, in various states of torture. Many of their faces look upward toward heaven, but there is one, Saint Anthony of Padua, who gazes straight down into my face. He holds the Christ child in one arm, and offers a loaf to a kneeling beggar with the other hand. His tender brown eyes see me. *Reggie*, he says.

Saint Anthony of Padua is a gentle presence, giving a loaf to the beggar. He does not have to get nailed to a cross.

•

Sister Maria del Rey has said that we should come to her with any Communion questions. I go at lunchtime. When she sees how much I am shaking, she looks concerned.

"Sister, can I receive Saint Anthony instead of Jesus Christ?" I ask.

Her eyes open wide and her mouth drops. She sends me back outside onto the playground for recess.

That afternoon in class Sister teaches us the song "I'm a Soldier in Christ's Army." I sing as loud as I can and try to catch her eye. I sense that she hears me and knows I want her attention, but she refuses to look at me.

Maybe I cannot marry Saint Anthony. Maybe I can only marry Jesus. But worse than the tortured heart Jesus wears for all to see is the fact that his suffering is meant to repeat all the time. It seems as if it is over when he is resurrected, but it isn't. It is all going to happen again.

•

I tell Kim that in the months my mother lived after my father's suicide, she often could not hear us when we spoke to her. She stared, her pupils small as pinpoints, as if something bright hung on the air before her.

"There is a story there," Kim says. "If you trace out how this came to happen, the ghosts will probably stop."

But I have not been able to see any order. The connective tissue between memories has been destroyed in the blasts. I worry that without cause and effect there is no story. I fail to connect the dots. Eventually, Kim stops asking me to try.

•

After *Moonchildren*, I'm cast in a big production of *The Music Man*. I play Zaneeta Shinn, the mayor's daughter. In a purple silk-and-taffeta dress, I twirl as I dance then run downstage and cry out, "Ye gods!"

•

When Tracy feels better enough to get up again, she is twenty pounds thinner. She is mad at me and won't live with me anymore, even though David has moved out and we could have the entire big place to ourselves. She finds a tiny one-room apartment behind Bicycle World on Cerrillos Road, around the corner from Manhattan Avenue, and gets an after-school job at the Oil and Gas accounting division on Alameda.

•

On a fall day our family drives to a place called Eagle
Nest, northeast of Santa Fe, and stops at the edge of a wild
expanse of meadow. While Sheila joins Jerry to search a
stretch of dry road for arrowheads, Tracy and I pretend to
ride horses in the high grass, galloping far, then pulling on
imaginary reins, rearing back and neighing, before setting
off again at a canter. We are each both horse and rider.

·

It is still daylight. I drive south on Cerrillos and turn the
corner to go past our old house.

The trees are gone.

I feel sick, a taste of iron surging up into my mouth.
The site where each tree stood is ruptured, scarred.

I press the gas and drive past, but circle back and park.
I want to jump from the car, run to the door, and scream
at the people now living there, but my hand hovers at the
door handle. The anger turns into something heavy that
sinks down my spine.

The uprooted ground is parched, already turning back
into desert.

·

Sheila calls me. Kathy's parents fight all the time. The
night before, they locked her in her room. She heard bottles breaking in the hall. I tell her to get her things, that
I'm coming to pick her up.

Mid-High, where she goes to ninth grade, is only a few blocks' walk from Manhattan Avenue. We call Uncle Bob and tell him why Sheila left Kathy's, and that she'll be living with me now.

I am determined I will be better to Sheila than I was to Tracy. I just cashed my social security check, so we go to the Saint Vincent DePaul Society and she picks out a nice bedspread for the mattress. I get a table and chairs for the main room, where we can eat and do homework. I take her to Vip's Big Boy for hamburgers.

My high school friend Kerry, who has gone to college in the Midwest, has left her cat, Layla, and a begonia plant for me to care for. Sheila attaches herself to Layla, and sleeps with her at night.

•

Shelia is home from school, but Layla is not here.

"She'll come home," I reassure her.

She walks back and forth in front of the house and along the side, calling again and again, "Layla!"

I go around the neighborhood with her and ask people if they've seen a cat, but no one has.

•

I forget to pay the bill and the electricity is turned off. It's dark, so we use candles and Sheila has to do her homework by the light of a flashlight.

Layla has not come home. "You hardly ever fed her," Sheila says.

"I did!" I insist, giving her a pleading look.

"Not enough. And you shouldn't have let her out. You were supposed to take care of her."

That night when I am in bed, she comes in and says, "I'm cold. Can I sleep with you?"

I let her come in with me. As she tries to get comfortable, she tells me she's hungry. There's not much in the house to eat. She pushes against me, kicks and whimpers. In the middle of the night it sounds as if she's crying, but when I touch her I can feel that she is deep asleep.

•

I have a long rehearsal and get home late. Sheila comes in carrying the flashlight and asks if she can sleep with me again, but I tell her I want to sleep alone.

I get up and give her a coat to wear and cover her up in her bed. We stand the flashlight up on the floor to be her night-light.

I try to think of things to make it up to her. Maybe I will buy some ice cream, but I remember that there is no electricity, so the refrigerator isn't working. I can't go and pay the electricity bill until I get my social security check, so another week and a half will have to go by in the dark.

•

There is a party at the governor's mansion thrown in honor of the theater's patron, Greer Garson. I drink glasses of champagne and pile a little plate high with prawns and smoked salmon canapés. When I've had enough, I fill my cloth purse with food for Sheila, more salmon and shrimp, pineapple wrapped in bacon, and chunks of cheese, avoiding the mysterious gray pâtés.

I see the governor's wife watching me from across the table, but I feel tipsy and don't care. I keep wrapping things in napkins and dumping them into my purse, meatballs, canapés, small squares of fruit bread, and cookies.

As I drive home through darkness on the Española highway, approaching headlights blur and multiply.

•

The next morning Sheila and I are eating a breakfast from my purse full of canapés, wiping caviar from shortbread cookies and chocolate from smoked salmon.

I notice that Kerry's plant looks dead, the leaves almost completely brown. In the past weeks, whenever I meant to water it, I never did. I tell myself to get up and fill a glass with water now and pour it in. But I stay where I am. I do not understand why doing such a small thing feels so hard. I am hoping that Sheila will notice and water it, but I cannot seem even to mention it to her.

•

After learning the Angelus in the first grade, I teach it to Tracy and Sheila and decide to stage the annunciation as a play.

Hands pressed in prayer, Tracy kneels on a folded blanket, a towel on her head as a veil. The room is dark, with a little light coming from the hallway. She whispers very quiet gibberish to make the sound of praying.

I turn on the closet light and she squints. Sheila kneels down before her, arms held out wide like wings.

"The angel of the Lord declared unto Mary!" I say.

Tracy bows her head, taps at her heart with her fist, and responds: "Be it done unto me according to thy word."

•

I stand with Tracy at the end of the hall, and she tells me that Sheila woke that morning and saw Mom holding a gun in the doorway of her room, staring at her.

I ask her where Mom could have gotten it. She doesn't know. "Where is it now?" I ask.

"Jerry found it in Mom's drawer," she says. "He buried it at the rodeo grounds."

Tracy tries to stop me but I pull loose and run down the hall to confront Mom, whom I find in the kitchen in her pajamas.

She tries to get away from me, but I block her passage from the room. I am taller than she is by several inches.

"A gun? Don't you know what a terrible thing that is that Sheila saw you with a gun?"

She tries to push past.

"Listen to me," I say.

She keeps trying to go, but I keep stopping her. I grasp hold of her shoulders and she doesn't resist. She stands before me panting, staring past me.

"What's wrong with you?" I yell, trying to make her react, but there's no anger in her.

Her shoulders soften and she escapes like she is made of slippery, malleable stuff. It is a strange sensation, not being able to hold on to her.

"Wait," I scream as she rushes up the hall to her room and locks the door.

My sisters are furious with me. "You make everything worse."

•

We share the flashlight at the table—Sheila's doing homework and I'm trying to write a paper for class. Shifting in my chair, I kick a ball with a bell in it from under the table. It rolls across the floor, jingling.

"Layla!" Sheila cries. She jumps up and shoots the beam of the flashlight all over the floor and under the chairs.

But soon she realizes that it is not Layla, only the cat toy dislodged from where it was hidden. She stands still, breathing hard, her jaw tight.

"You didn't take care of Layla!" she screams. "You're a selfish bitch!"

She runs into the front room and smashes the oval window on the door with the flashlight, then throws the flashlight against the wall, the batteries dropping out and rolling on the wood. Except for a little light coming in from the street, everything is dark.

"My hand is bleeding," she cries.

"Let me see," I say.

"Get away!" she yells and runs out the door, slamming it so more glass falls. She goes left near Cerrillos Road, toward Tracy's apartment.

•

Tracy comes for some of Sheila's books and clothes. She has brought her own flashlight. "We'll come back and get the rest tomorrow. She's better off with me," Tracy says. Tracy's apartment behind Bicycle World is a third of the size of a single room on Manhattan Avenue.

I sit on the floor in the dark. Every time a car drives by, its headlights cause the broken glass to glimmer.

•

I am afraid to read *The Marriage of Heaven and Hell*, but I dare myself to look at William Blake's drawings. I sit in the college library with a large book of his etchings open before me, images composed of gradient shadows and white rays that suggest intense brightness.

In one he depicts God with cloven hooves and a snake wrapped around his body, stretching horizontally on the air over a dreaming man.

•

Sheila's left some things in the room she's vacated: an almost empty package of Oreos and a notebook with notes from her world history class. Skimming through the pages, I stop when I read the words: *Mom and I are a Venn diagram.* Two circles intersect, almost eclipsing each other, with small areas on either side where they do not touch. On the left it says *Me*. On the right, *Mom*. The big area in the middle that is both of them is shaded with pencil.

I put the notebook down. I want to leave the room, but my legs won't move. The window shrinks down to the size of a postage stamp.

•

At noon on a Saturday, Tom knocks on my door. As we walk downtown, I talk about Tracy and Sheila and how mad they are at me. He listens, but doesn't say very much. He takes me to the Forge, a dark bar on Alameda Street, and we drink beer.

When we get back to Manhattan Avenue, we are laughing, slurring our words, and anxious to get to my bed. We make love, and afterward, just before he falls asleep, he tells me that he won't be coming back to Santa Fe after this semester is over. I shake him, tell him to wake up, that I want to talk. He stirs himself a little bit, but can't keep his eyes open. In a groggy voice, just before he goes to sleep, he mentions a drama school on the East Coast.

I sit up and stare at him, studying the smoothness of his skin as if I'm trying to memorize it. With the sunlight through the window, his hair has a gold cast to it.

•

At the Stuckey's roadside store near Camel Rock, Mom and Dad buy us each a small souvenir in the gift shop. Sheila picks a lucky rabbit's foot.

Riding home in the car, she lets me hold it. I feel bones under the fur.

"They must have killed a real rabbit to get this," I say.

A shadow comes over her little freckled face and I regret saying it. She takes it back from me. "That's okay," she says. She thinks about what I've said and I know she doesn't like it. "That's okay," she says again, clutches it in one hand, and looks out the car window.

•

When my social security check comes I cash it and pay the electricity bill, then wander into Woolworth's on the

Santa Fe Plaza. I run out of money every month way before I should, and I've told myself to be more practical,
but right now I don't care. I am intent on buying gifts for
my sisters.

Feigning interest in an eyelash curler, I stand eaves-
dropping in the cosmetics aisle as a plump Navajo girl,
about fourteen, tries to persuade her mother to buy her
a silvery white lipstick. It feels like a tease the way the
mother stays there looking at it but keeps saying no.

In other aisles in the store, I search for things for my
sisters.

I stand in line at the cash register with a bottle of
Wind Song for Sheila, a new watermelon Lip Smacker
for Tracy, and two cotton blouses with eyelet at the neck-
lines, one for each of them.

The woman in front of me is buying a small plaid
dress and a package of hairclips with ducklings on them.

I am also buying gifts for my daughters, I say to myself
as I dig out a twenty-dollar bill and wait to pay.

•

When I bring them the gifts, my sisters allow me to stay.

Tracy tells me that she's called Uncle Bob and told
him that Sheila is living with her.

"He's fine with it," she says.

"Even though you're only seventeen?"

She shrugs. "Yes."

The apartment behind Bicycle World is as small as a closet.

•

Tracy has bought a used VW Bug and drives Sheila to school every morning before she drives to Santa Fe High. Tracy organizes things for them with an efficiency that stuns me. She manages to keep a little food in their refrigerator: a bowl of tuna fish, a loaf of bread, some cheese. On the narrow kitchen counter there's a cutting board and a heavy wooden rolling pin. Sometimes when I come over, Tracy makes good, thin tortillas in a cast-iron pan, perfectly browning them.

•

I hate going back to the empty apartment on Manhattan Avenue and hesitate before the door, which looks taller than usual and seems to lean slightly toward me. The knob is cold, and the door creaks as I open it. After I've closed the door and taken a few steps into the apartment, I hear it creak again.

I sit doing homework and feel something observing me.

•

Nanny reads to me, Jerry, Tracy, and Sheila from a picture book, while we stare at the illustration. A tall lady all in white with white light all around her is suspended on the air, while the children of Fátima kneel on the ground looking up at her, afraid.

"Fear not! I will not harm you," Nanny reads. "I am from heaven!"

•

When Tracy graduates, she and Sheila move to Albuquerque. Tracy registers at UNM, and she registers Sheila for Highland High School. I visit them a few days after they move. They have a furnished two-bedroom apartment not far from Jerry's. Tracy has hung a poster of Al Pacino as Serpico over her bed, and Sheila has one of a hermit holding a lamp, the words *Stairway to Heaven* written on it in calligraphic script.

In the bathroom, they have a collection of dime-store lipsticks and perfumes.

•

I am cast as Cassandra in *The Trojan Women*. At the first rehearsal I stand downstage with my hand on my throat, and prophesize my own murder.

•

Rehearsals prevent me from waitressing at night after classes. The rent is too high living alone on Manhattan Avenue, so I go to see a studio apartment in the back of an old house on Galisteo Street.

Large windows and a cement floor give the main room a bright chill. The walls are grayish-beige linoleum with a faux wood grain, and peeling at the corners near the ceiling.

As I go up the two heavy cement steps into the kitchen, a shadow looms to the left. For the split second before I turn, I am certain a man is standing there, but sigh with relief when I see a doorless closet with a few planks of wood as shelving.

The bathroom, with mustard-yellow walls, is through the kitchen, just beyond a narrow, archaic-looking oven standing crooked on short iron legs. There is no shower, only an old, deep, claw-footed tub, paint peeling inside. A window with casement and latch still visible and a cabinet with its lock still in place are both sealed shut and painted over. Everywhere is evidence of crude room divisions, forcibly executed. In the narrow confines of this bathroom, the air is heavy and hard to breathe. I sense hopelessness and imagine a mistreated girl dying here.

I decide against moving in, but as I am leaving, I run into a friend, Penny, from the department. She lives in a tiny house just behind and shares the long driveway that runs right past the entrance to the apartment. She encourages me to move in. She knows I have occasional trouble with my car. "I can always give you rides to the college if you need them," she says.

She goes in with me to look at the place again. While she's with me, it doesn't feel so awful. It is ninety-five dollars a month, and I decide that the main room, spacious and filled with light, and Penny being nearby make everything okay.

•

After moving in, I sit up at night with the lights on bright, trying to read. I hear a soft hiss and smell a vaguely sulfurous odor, like someone has just lit a match. I worry that this place is a tinderbox for enchantments.

•

There is a high wall outside along the driveway. From over that wall I have heard two female voices speaking Spanish. Between words, one warbles like a bird and sometimes whistles, while the other, in a hoarse, low-pitched croak, spits her words and makes grunting sounds.

When I ask Penny about this, she tells me that a strange mother and daughter live in that house. She shakes her head. "One would be lost without the other."

Their proximity makes me feel worse. I worry that their insanity is infectious, and that I might breathe it in through the air from the open window. But there are times when I feel a fascinated revulsion. I sometimes stand quietly near the screen of my open door and listen for sounds from them. There is something I might understand here if I listen hard enough, a knot I might unravel.

•

For Nanny's funeral card, my mother chooses a picture of the child martyr Saint Agnes embracing a lamb. There are four or five copies of the card left in different places in the house. On the back they say: "Blessed are they that mourn, for they shall be comforted."

•

On the yellow pad, to the side of the grocery list, my mother has written: *Queen of Mercy*.

•

Besides dolls dressed as nuns, Tracy and I have statues of the Blessed Virgin Mary, little gifts Mom brings home. They are all over our room: between two books on a shelf, on the nightstand or windowsill, facing in random directions, mixed into a box of toys and Barbies. We use them in sacrilegious ways, to play the roles of neighbors to our other dolls. They always play lonely women. They are sometimes mean. We feel a little guilty using them this way.

•

I knock a statue of the Blessed Virgin Mary off the shelf and one of her hands breaks off at the wrist. I look all over the room for the hand and cannot find it and wonder if there has been an assumption, the assumption of the hand of the Virgin into heaven.

She becomes my favorite, the one with the missing hand.

•

One of Nanny's funeral cards is on the floor near the nightstand. My mother is bleary-eyed, weaving, barely sitting up straight in her bed. She is using the pillow as a typewriter.

•

I ask my father once, when I am eleven or twelve, if we will ever visit Ireland.

"No," he replies, taken aback. The impression I have from the silence that follows is that it is too rarefied and unreachable a place.

•

Every Easter Sunday, Mom roasts a leg of lamb. It has a particular pungent smell that fills the house, a smell I associate with resurrection.

Mom has read about a way to make potatoes bake faster by driving a big nail lengthwise through the center. When the potatoes are finished, it is dangerous to take out the nails. I watch as Mom, holding each potato with an oven mitt, extracts the blazing nails with the tines of a fork.

While we eat, the nails lie on a plate on the counter, heat rising from them in little gusts.

·

As the prophetess Cassandra I come onstage each night in absolute darkness, carrying a burning torch. The part that burns is fashioned of rags soaked in kerosene. A prop man stands backstage with me before my entrance and lights it on fire. I enter in a trance, holding the heavy thing aloft. Downstage I stand gazing up high into the great dark gulf of the universe, and pray to Apollo, describing the vision of my death.

To my right, my mother, Hecuba, stands weeping because she believes I have gone mad. She sends the herald Talthybius to take the torch from me and he carries it away.

"Mother! My mother!" I call out to her. "Crown my triumph with a wreath."

·

I'm sitting at the table trying to write a paper for school when I sense that something, someone, is lying very still on my mattress. I know it is a *she*. The air feels silky with this fact. She does not want to hurt me. She doesn't threaten me.

I sit frozen, unable to move, and as if to snap me out of my paralysis, the refrigerator in the kitchen shifts on and hums, a low, steady rumble.

I know who she is. I stand, but I won't look at her. She is me, deflated and tired with her eyes closed, lying on her back under the covers. I would go to her and smooth her hair and tell her that everything is all right, as if she were a younger sibling, except that I might discover that she is cold, that she is not breathing. Or even worse, she might be cold, not breathing, and then suddenly open her eyes.

•

"A lot of help you are!" Mom screams at the framed picture of the Blessed Mother in her room and throws an ashtray at it. The glass cracks and the picture slides off the wall onto its side near her nightstand.

Susie's license tags jingle as she waddles out of the room and finds a table to hide under.

Mom hasn't slept for two nights.

There has been a story in the news of an actress who tried to kill herself by drinking Drano. Mom threatens to drink the Drano kept in the kitchen cabinet. Tracy, Jerry, and I run ahead, trying to prevent her from getting to the cabinet. While Sheila moves in circles, fretting and crying in the kitchen doorway, Mom keeps fighting us, pushing against us.

"Your father doesn't have the guts to kill me, so I'll have to do it myself!"

We yell at her that we love her. We don't know if hearing this helps her or upsets her.

She is strong for someone so tired, someone who can barely walk. I grab her arm as it strains, reaching for the Drano, but she clutches my hand with her other one, so hard I hear something crack, and I struggle to get away from her. Sheila grabs hold of Mom and pulls her.

"Mommy!" she keeps crying.

Jerry blocks her, but even he can hardly hold his own against her, even with the three of us trying to keep her back. I think of calling Dad at work, but I'm afraid to move away, and I wonder if Dad being here would help or make things worse.

It goes on. It goes on and on, until she lets out a strange, broken sigh and retreats to her room.

Jerry grabs the car keys. He is going to meet his friends. I give him the bottle of Drano and tell him to throw it away somewhere far from this house. Tracy, Sheila, and I turn on the television and look for something funny to watch. I know Mom is finished for the night, but I see uncertainty in both my sisters' faces. They are listening for footsteps in the hall.

"She's not gonna come out again tonight."

They look at me, and I say it again. Tracy turns the channels until she finds *F Troop*.

•

I hear from someone at school that one of Kim's movies, *The Goddess*, a black-and-white film from the early sixties, is playing at the small art cinema, the Bijou.

I go during the day to see it. Kim is vivacious in the beginning and looks young and slim and beautiful. But the story becomes very dark.

At her mother's funeral, standing all in black, with a little black veil hanging from a hat around her face, she cries out in anguish and loses her balance. Supported by others, she gives herself over to a guttural wail, an unfettered expression of grief that hits me like a blow at the base of my spine. The character has a breakdown.

I return to my apartment and keep the door and window open, listening for voices from over the wall.

•

I think of Blake's depiction of God, a horizontal figure in the air, wrapped in a snake.

•

I open a side cabinet beneath the kitchen sink that I thought was soldered shut like some of the cabinets in the bathroom. Inside along with soiled rags and desiccated lumps of steel wool, I see an old bottle of Drano.

I freeze. I am turning inside out, my memories taking form around me. The rusty steel wool looks like knotted mats of bloody hair, the aftermath of a violent death. I reach in, intending to take it all out, to get rid of it so I don't have to live with it here, but can't bring myself to touch any of it. Shaking, I close the cabinet.

A faint chord of dissonant music, like someone running her fingers across the strings of a harp, sounds above me on the air. Sweat breaks out on my forehead and the back of my neck.

•

I am lying in bed. A man materializes near the stairs to the kitchen, bowing slightly forward. His hair, which stands on end, glows, lit flecks rising like embers and ashes. He endures the pain of the fire. I sit up and he senses me looking at him and begins to lift his head, though it seems to hurt him to do so. I lie back down, my body quaking, and squeeze my eyes shut. I remember my father telling me that William Blake saw angels with fiery hair. I try to persuade myself that it is an angel.

The cut worm forgives the plow. The cutting, I tell myself over and over, is not still going on.

•

I am too nervous to stay in my apartment. Instead, I get out of bed, get in my car, and drive. It starts to rain. I park on a road off the highway near the junction, the rain hitting the windshield and the hood of the car in a hard torrent. I can make out the blur of passing headlights. Even in its violence, the rain soothes me. I told my mother often when I was little how much I loved rain and she always replied by telling me that I belonged in Ireland. I wonder why my family did not leave New Mexico, and why it was that Ireland felt like an unachievable dream.

•

I sell my car and buy a plane ticket one way across the Atlantic.

PART THREE

I stand at the prow of the boat as it pushes through night-dark water.

This morning I was in London, then took a train to Swansea, Wales, where I got on this ferry to Cobh Harbor. This dark is different from the dark everywhere else in the world. It is Irish dark. The sea is Irish, the wind, the dampness. I never belonged in the immense, arid barrenness of New Mexico, with its dry red rock canyons. How clear that is to me in this moment. If I ever go back there, I cannot imagine it will be for many years. I'm almost home now, almost in the greener world of bogs and mist.

It is 4:00 AM and the other passengers are inside sleeping, the lights switched low in the cabin. I think that

I can tell someone, and it will be true, that I am homeless. I sold my car, got rid of almost everything else, which had not been much. It thrills and terrifies me to be so free.

I press my hand against the scarf around my neck, and feel it rippling in the gale. It is the only thing I have left that once belonged to my mother, inexpensive, almost transparent beige, nothing of particular beauty. I borrowed it from her when I was thirteen and never remembered to give it back. It was in my drawer among my things for so long I ignored it, until my mother's death, when it took on the significance of an heirloom. And I have in my purse a copy of *The Wind Among the Reeds*, one of my father's favorite books by Yeats.

As dawn arrives, I can see Cobh Harbor ahead, the infamous place of departure where, during the famine, the coffin ships left for America.

I am almost in Ireland, and the closer I get, the more I feel the proximity of my parents. Too nervous and excited, I have not slept for several nights and as the sun appears at the edge of the horizon I believe in the miraculous. The wind beats hard and my mother's scarf loosens. I grasp it just as it starts to fly away, and hold it aloft, watch it ripple in the wind. But then I let go, and the wind takes it, carrying it in the air. It settles on the water and soon becomes invisible. I touch my neck. It feels bare, and I realize I no longer have anything that belonged to either of them. The copy of *The Wind Among the Reeds* in my purse did not belong to my father, though it is the same edition as the one he owned.

I imagine my mother's scarf moving unseen gracefully down into the chambers of the sea. I want it back. Something I can hold, an object no matter how measly, anything, a button, a piece of lint from one of their pockets.

•

I remember the little blue moon-shaped bottle. *Je reviens*, I think to myself as the ferry reaches the harbor. *I shall return to you.*

•

It is a mild spring afternoon, my first day in Dublin, and the sky is a mix of sun and clouds. I lug my big plaid suitcase toward a worn-looking brick house, four floors high, a bed-and-breakfast called Fatima House on Upper Gardiner Street.

A petite woman with long straight red hair, her bangs in pin curls around her forehead, half opens the door and surveys my face and demeanor with a fierce, eagle-eyed expression. After a moment of hesitation, she seems to decide in my favor, and lets me in.

"You're traveling alone?"

"Yes."

"On holiday?"

"Not exactly. I'll be moving to Dublin."

She squints into my face. "Are you Catholic?"

I eye the crucifix around her neck, and reply that I am.

She nods and introduces herself as Mrs. Cleary. I pay her in pound notes, which she receives with a dignified nervousness.

She helps me carry my suitcase up an enormous, drafty staircase and leads me to a room that faces Upper Gardiner Street. She pushes the curtains open farther; I look away from the dust motes moving in new light. She gives me the key. "Breakfast begins at seven and ends at half nine," she says as she leaves, closing the door behind her.

The furniture is gray and beige like the bedspreads, the prim Victorian wallpaper, bloated in spots from what looks like decades of damp. The iron bars on the headboards remind me of something that might be in an asylum. Alone, I feel a sudden panic squeeze my stomach. I have a few names scribbled on a torn piece of loose-leaf paper by a musician I met in school who had been in Ireland a few years before. He had no addresses or phone numbers to go with the names. "You don't need them in Ireland," he'd said. "You go to the local pubs and ask for people." I retrieve the scrap of paper from my purse. *McDaids—Harry Street.*

I throw the door open and rush after Mrs. Cleary as she is descending the stairs and ask if she'll give me directions to McDaids.

•

I follow my father outside to the car. The sky is a cold silvery blue, a hush over everything.

"You see those birds gathering?" he asks, pointing to a telephone wire along Siringo Road. More birds land on the wire.

"Why do they do that?" I ask.

"They feel the snow coming. They like to watch it fall."

"How can they feel it? Can they feel the molecules coming?"

He laughs. "The air changes, so yes, there must be molecules to that change."

Christmas lights glow in all the store windows as we drive along Cerrillos Road. "Light has molecules, doesn't it?" I ask.

When he says that he thinks it does, I ask if when a light goes out, it leaves molecules behind.

"For a while, I think," he says.

•

I open the door to McDaids and a wave of noise floods out onto the street, the single room of the establishment vibrating with laughter and yelling.

Daylight filters in a big front window and through a heavy veil of cigarette smoke. I hold the piece of paper up to the bartender, who is filling a line of pint glasses at the tap.

"The only name I know is Mike O'Donnell," he yells over the noise, "but haven't seen him in a year."

With nowhere to go, I head back toward Upper Gardiner Street, as groups of small black-and-white birds fly over the river and begin assembling on the roofs beyond O'Connell Bridge. I wander over the bridges and the streets along the quays, hoping that someone—maybe a young man—will recognize my essential Irishness and approach me; that there will be little I'll need to explain about myself.

I go to places I think this young man might go. I walk to the campus of Trinity College and sit in the quadrangle reading *The Wind Among the Reeds*, the title a sign to this man, who will almost certainly be a literary person. People stroll by but do not address me and I don't make eye contact.

When I arrive back at Fatima House that evening, Mrs. Cleary meets me in the foyer, where she is switching on a lamp, and sees me holding my copy of *The Wind Among the Reeds*.

"My husband is from a small village in Sligo, near Yeats country," she says.

I've heard the phrase *Yeats country* before from my father, but for some reason thought it referred to a territory of the mind; the dreamscape of Yeats's poems.

"Is it beautiful?" I ask. "Yeats country?"

"Oh yes," she says, and goes on to describe hazel woods and lakes.

When I ask her how far it is she tells me it is "all the way across Ireland and a bit to the north." "All the way across" sounds far, the way she said it, and somehow that impression stays with me. *Yeats country.* The words glow in my mind as I climb the dark staircase to my room.

•

Dad likes finding me sitting in a corner reading his wrinkled copies of Yeats or Dylan Thomas, and one day brings me a journal to write my own poems in.

•

Father Godfrey, the tall, gangly Franciscan friar who wears black plastic glasses with Coke-bottle lenses, comes to the classroom and tells us that we are lambs of God, and that the sacrament of Confirmation will be another step toward our salvation. We each need to pick another name, a saint's name. I know in an instant that my name will be Barbara.

•

The Grand Canyon will be our first big vacation. We will stay in a fancy lodge on the edge of the canyon. Mom is excited to go horseback riding. It will be one of the first things we do when we get there. The trail rides we've gone on in New Mexico have not allowed Mom to gallop her horse, but she makes calls and finds out that there are trail rides at the Grand Canyon that allow a mix of new riders and experienced ones. "I'll get a spirited horse," she says, proud of her ability as an equestrian. "A horse can feel what you're feeling," she explains. "If it senses your confidence, it will respect you."

•

Mrs. Cleary has taken to knocking on my door, coming in, and sitting down on the edge of the bed to complain about unwed mothers in Ireland, and the loose morals of people who come to stay under her roof. She asks me to call her Theresa.

People often ring the bell downstairs and she turns them away saying she is full, but most all of the rooms are empty, the doors wide open.

"I pick and choose," she says. "I never let the ones with the backpacks in. Why can't they use suitcases like respectable people?"

"Did you let me stay because I didn't have a backpack?" I ask.

"Yes, but mostly it was your eyes. I'm good at reading faces, although sometimes I make a mistake and let a heathen stay and then find myself cleaning up their vodka bottles."

•

I buy postcards with pictures of the Book of Kells at Trinity College and write one for each of my sisters and my brother.

I ask Mrs. Cleary where I can mail them and she informs me that there is a postal strike in Ireland that has been going on for months.

"You take a chance by mailing them. They'll likely not get through."

It registers for the first time how far away I am from my sisters and brother.

•

The movie *Ryan's Daughter*, which was filmed years earlier in the West of Ireland, is in an extended residence at the cinema near Parnell Square. Waiting for the box office to open, I see a guy around my age wearing Levis and a windbreaker, and I peg him for an American. I approach him and we start to talk.

Fred is from Illinois and we sit together at the movie and afterward we go to a crowded neighborhood pub for a drink.

"You came all this way with only the name of a pub to go to?" he asks.

I nod, embarrassed.

"I can't believe you're staying in a bed-and-breakfast alone in Dublin when you could be seeing the beauties of western Ireland and meeting people from all over the world."

He tells me that he doesn't like Dublin, that he's only here because he's going to take the ferry to Wales and then to London to fly back to the States.

"The West is the reason people come to Ireland!" He tells me about the Killarney Youth Hostel, a beautiful building that looks like a Swiss chalet, situated on a green hillside.

"I'd like to go to Yeats country," I say.

"But first you should go to Killarney. It's the nerve center for people traveling in the West. From there you can find people to travel north with you to Yeats country."

•

In Killarney I befriend Swedes, Italians, Germans, Australians, and in keeping with everyone else, exchange my unwieldy plaid suitcase for a large, bright yellow backpack, which can be left in safekeeping at the hostel while I go with others to see the local attractions. Because it's so close to the Gulf Stream, the area, replete with lakes, lush and intensely green, feels almost tropical, the high trees filled with screeching birds with wild calls.

In a little shop on the grounds of Muckross House, an old estate house of castle-like proportions at Killarney National Park, there are postcards of many of Ireland's attractions. I buy some of Yeats country: one of swans in early morning light; one of Classiebawn Castle in an effulgence of mist; one of the hill, Ben Bulben, in evening light after a storm; one of hazel woods; and one of Yeats himself sitting with his dog. And postcards with pictures of the lakes of Killarney for my sisters and brother.

I write them but cannot send them. I will wait for the postal strike to end, although no one can predict when that might happen.

•

I eat breakfast with Gwen and Anne, two Englishwomen in their midtwenties who work as physical therapists in London.

Our conversation is interrupted by the loud voice of an arrogant American at a nearby table. We shake our heads and roll our eyes.

"Well," red-haired Gwen says, "he is obnoxious, but I do think he's kind of attractive. Don't you?"

I shake my head no. "He's a jock."

They both look at me confused.

"There's only one definition I know for that word," Anne says.

After a beat, the three of us burst into laughter.

I ask them if they want to travel with me to Yeats country. Their time is limited and they can't go that far north, but invite me to join them on a three- or four-day excursion by bicycle around the Dingle Peninsula, a thirty-mile stretch west of Killarney, high rocky cliffs, glacial valleys, and prehistoric remains.

Leaving our packs at the hostel, we take only what we need, and within two hours are riding westward on winding pathways through small fields with thatched cottages, veering sometimes toward stretches of wild, uncultivated land overlooking the sea. Daisies and fuchsia grow thick along some of the narrower routes and byways. Cars rarely pass, but the occasional ramshackle lorry rattles by, some carrying big metal canisters to be filled with milk. Flocks of black-faced sheep have the right-of-way and we pull off to the side to let them pass. The light keeps changing in the sky, the hills alternately bright and in shadow. We ride for an hour before it begins to rain. We scale a hill to a small, isolated hotel overlooking Inch Strand. The rain keeps on so we decide to spend the night. We check in, store our bicycles, then take our packs upstairs to a room with three single beds. I go down ahead of the other two to the hotel restaurant and sit near a window, a vast view of the sea from up on this cliff. It moves in one great, subtle undulation, the raindrops disrupting the smooth waves of its surface, so it seems to shiver.

Two figures in raincoats, a man and a woman, walk on the sand below holding hands, shielding their faces against the wet. From this distance, they could be my parents.

·

When the rain stops, the girls and I walk along the strand, gulls shrieking in the strong wind. The bodies of two sheep are pushed onto the shore as the tide comes in, their coats sodden with seawater. Their eyes are closed, but they appear unharmed, like they're asleep. The water begins to pull them back to sea.

"How strange," Gwen says.

When the tide pushes them again onto the sand, I avert my eyes and look ahead on a break in the clouds, where rays of white light shoot down into the water. The shrieking of the gulls intensifies as the water rushes away. I turn and see a young man in the distance on a sandy bank. I wonder if he is real. Shielding my eyes from the wind, I try to focus on him. His longish, tangled hair moves against his face. The closer he gets, the more handsome he appears to be, tall with prominent cheekbones, and a relaxed, full mouth, his eyes ice blue, gleaming and fervent.

His faded, dark green jacket with cloth buttons looks like it was once formal wear. It is fitted to him, but tight across the chest and shoulders, and his pants are worn and his boots muddy.

"I'm Nevan," he says, peering at me and ignoring the others.

"Regina," I say.

"Regina Cæli, the Queen of Heaven."

I smile, repressing a thrilled and awkward laugh.

Gwen and Anne seem nervous, maybe because of his disheveled clothing, but his presence excites me.

They are his sheep in the tide, he explains, his Kerry accent easier to understand than that of the other locals

I've met. "They break a fence," he says, pointing to a nearby headland. "When they get very close to the edge of the cliff, they get the urge to jump."

•

The next three days are bright and nearly cloudless. I am the slowest cyclist of the three, Gwen and Anne often waiting ahead at a distance for me to catch up.

We pass farmers with donkeys or blunt plows on the fields, and women in shawls, driving calves along the road. We stop in various towns to buy bread, tomatoes, and cheese from little shops, then sit and eat on hills facing the beach, or in meadows near running brooks. Gwen knows the names of the wildflowers: bluebell, foxglove, heather.

In whatever wild, windy, lonely place we hike or cycle, my breath ragged from riding or climbing hard, I imagine Nevan appearing in the distance.

Huddling and shivering in a small tent battered by wind, we camp one night on Slea Head, at the tip of the peninsula. In the morning we visit prehistoric stone huts at the edge of the sea, then travel north to wild beaches outside Ballyferriter, the farthest westerly point on the mainland.

We stop our bikes on a roadside with a view of three hill cliffs, grass like yellow-green velvet covering the tops that sweep upward before falling sheer, in jagged rock, hundreds of feet down to the sea, where the water foams hard and gannets flee the splashing waves.

"These cliffs are called the Three Sisters," Gwen says, holding tight to the map, which flutters in the wind. I ask Anne to take a photograph of me with the cliffs in the background. After the postal strike ends, I will send it to Tracy and Sheila.

My sisters are at the forefront of my thoughts now. I blame the fierceness of the Atlantic winds for the tears streaking my face.

•

I said good-bye to Anne and Gwen at the Killarney Youth Hostel, and set out again for Inch Strand. After checking into the little hotel, I take off my jeans, T-shirt, and sweater and put on a blouse and long skirt. Walking back to the beach where I saw Nevan, the wind whips the skirt wildly at my legs.

I walk on the strand and climb a hill toward the headland that Nevan had pointed to. He is there with five or six sheep, guiding them into a fenced area. As it begins to rain, he spots me, and gestures to the sky, then beckons me.

"I was just going in for a cup of tea," he cries over the wind. I study the wide spread of his shoulders as I follow him down a hill to a cottage, which is set against a descent, protected from the ocean gales. He turns once and gives me a warm, flirtatious smile, and I smile back. The whitewashed structure appears ancient with slates on the roof and one nearly opaque window. He pulls the rough wood door open and we step inside where the dark air is cold, and smells of paraffin and some unnamable mustiness. My eyes struggle to adjust, the single window admitting almost no light. One wall is curved like it might buckle. The floor is earth.

Nevan pours water into a heavy black kettle that hangs from a crane, then stirs the embers beneath a layer of ash, reviving an old fire, and adds a new chunk of turf. The flames bristle, sending a spark airborne. In the sudden light, holy pictures appear over the mantel. I am surprised to see a portrait of John F. Kennedy.

A big stuffed chair with no legs, torn grayish upholstery covered in faded roses, faces the hearth. The fire now brightening, Nevan stands and brushes off his knees, and I notice that the ground all around him shimmers. He sees me looking and says, "Shattered glass. Ground down as fine as sand."

In a soft voice, he announces, "My mother died almost a year ago now. This room is very much the way she left it."

I wonder if it is meant as an apology for the state of things.

"The day my mother died, the mirror fell. One year," he whispers.

He points to the chair and I hesitate. I take a step back as if his mother is sitting there. He urges, "Sit," moving close and indicating the chair. I settle on its edge. He pulls up a cane chair and sits between me and the hearth.

On a table against the wall is an old wooden hairbrush, dark bristles matted with coarse gray-white hairs. A comb missing a few teeth, also fraught with the same gray-white hairs, lies next to it. A stub of candle stands between them, and just behind, a warped unframed picture of Christ leans against the wall. Crowned with thorns and embracing the crucifix, he lifts his eyes to heaven, irises drifted up so high they are hardly visible.

I look again at the brush. The hair has a gloss and resilience to it, a vague shimmer of oil like the hair on the head of someone living. A delicate, sour stink issues from the cushion of the chair beneath me. A nerve goes tight at the back of my neck.

I see Nanny's wizened face, slightly whiskered, her sunken chest rising and falling. I hear Nanny muttering under her breath.

Nevan clears his throat.

"Why didn't you clean up the broken mirror?" I ask.

He tenses at my question. The kettle begins to steam, but he makes no move to go to it.

He shakes his head. "I should have."

There is still a strain of hope in his voice when he says, "I've had this idea that someone would come. That a woman was going to arrive to this remote place."

A part of me holds back an incredulous laugh, wondering if he means that a woman would come and clean it up, but then I understand.

"A woman meant to be with me . . ." he continues. "When I saw you on the strand a few days back, I thought you might be . . ."

With every moment I feel myself closing off to him more. His pained inward smile becomes a grimace. He knows he is driving me away, but he doesn't seem to know how it has happened, how he has lost me.

The kettle trembles at the boil, steam hissing from its spout. He turns and looks at it as if it were reprimanding him.

He gets up, takes the kettle off the crane, and settles it in the shimmering earth around the hearth. He does not make tea, but just stands staring down at it with a surrendered smile.

"I think it's stopped raining," I say, rising to my feet, relieved to put air between myself and that cushion. He faces in my direction but doesn't look at me, his eyes on something just past my shoulder. I feel afraid, but not of him.

•

On a chilly night, my father sits in near darkness in the backyard looking up at a sky crowded with stars. When I go out and ask him what he is doing, he explains to me what constellations are.

"Do you see those very bright stars up there? That's the constellation Orion, the hunter. Can you see the bow and arrow?" he asks, his breath forming a cloud.

"I don't see the hunter," I say with frustration.

"Do you see those three bright stars all clustered together? That's Orion's belt, so even if you can't picture the rest of him, you know he's there in the sky when you see his belt."

Dad has a friend back in Yonkers named Jim O'Ryan. I ask him, "Is Orion the Irish constellation?"

He laughs, a high-pitched delighted laugh. "Maybe it should be," he says. After a silence, he laughs again.

The cold is biting. He notices I am shivering, takes off his jacket, and puts it over my shoulders. He sits back in the chair and I stand beside him. We see a star fall and streak the sky, and a pink one that moves a tiny bit, like it is shaking.

•

The wind is harsh as I set out on my way back to the Inch Hotel. My eyes fill with tears, blurring my vision. I see something ahead, being pushed in by the tide. It looks like Nanny, sodden in her old gray coat, her glasses cracked, her eyes open in my direction. It is like the sea has spit her up from its depths, and in spite of the wind all around me, I smell her—stale urine, Noxzema, menthol cigarette smoke.

I try not to look at the sheep as it ebbs in the tide.

•

Back at the Inch Hotel, I sleep with the light on. It must be two or three in the morning when the bulb flashes and goes out. I hear a low twang and vibration and I am no longer alone in the room. A figure stands at my bedside, waiting for me to look. I hide under the blanket, curling my body into a tight fist. I press my face into my pillow so as not to breathe it in. "No, no, no," I mutter through clenched teeth.

In the two weeks I've been in Ireland, I have kept the enchantments at bay, even at night. Even with the sad smells coming from the wallpaper and the old warped wooden dressers standing, waiting in the shadows, I have managed.

Hidden beneath the blanket, I am grateful for every sound outside the room: footsteps, the jingle of keys, someone coughing, a turning knob and a door squeaking open. I listen hard, these sounds holding me to the everyday world.

•

A deck of cards sits on a little table near Nanny's chair. She holds her cigarette in the air between two fingers.

•

When she comes home from work, my mother hugs me, and I lean against her, the vibrations between us very strong. I give the sensation a name: *doubling*. I explain to her, "There is the Trinity, which means three, the Father, Son, and Holy Ghost. They are three and one at the same time. And then there is the doubling, which is the mother and the daughter, who are two and one at the same time."

"You're a sweetheart," she says and kisses me on the forehead, then embraces me again. She is tired from work, and sighs into my hair.

•

Mom is looking at a picture in a magazine of a painting, a woman in a shawl wearing an expression that is both bold and thoughtful.

"Who is she?" I ask.

"Cathleen ni Houlihan," Mom says.

"But . . . who is that?"

Mom thinks a moment. "She's Ireland herself."

"Ireland is a woman?" I ask, amazed.

"Yes," Mom says, and laughs a little.

•

It is dawn, and when the morning light begins to filter in, the figure leaves. I fall into a deep sleep, and wake two hours later, raking the room with my eyes. I still sense the presence I thought had gone.

My stomach aches as I think of Nevan's mother's brush like something alive, the hair stuck within the bristles still growing. I think of Nanny's smell and how it filled the air of our house long after she died.

"Start at the beginning," Kim said when she wanted me to tell her what happened in my family, but I had no idea what the beginning was.

I hear the sea through the window, the steady drive as a tide pushes in. For the first time I think that maybe Nanny is the beginning. Maybe this answer has always been there, just under the surface. The tide retreats gradually, then forcefully returns.

•

I arrive back at the Killarney Youth Hostel, check in, go upstairs, choose a lower bunk in a large room filled with beds, slide my backpack beneath it, and fall into a shallow, uneasy sleep, relieved when young foreigners mill in and out, speaking in Nordic and European tongues.

It is afternoon when I get up. The enchantment is still not gone. I take out the postcards of Yeats country, the place where the silver and golden apples grow. Maybe the lit shroud of mist around Classiebawn Castle is really a kind of curtain, and if you pass through it you might find yourself in Tír na nÓg.

The book of Irish myths said that there are various entrances to the Otherworld. A woman once visited standing stones in County Mayo and disappeared from her mortal life without a trace.

If I can just get to Yeats country.

•

My mother and Nanny have a terrible fight. My mother yells at my father and sends him to the store. I go with him and after we get the things we've been sent out for, my father pulls into the parking lot of Manny's Lounge. As I wait, the snow gathers. The wind blows against the car and when my father comes out, snow has blanketed the entire windshield and I am shivering.

When we get home, I stand in the front yard looking up, the snow stinging my face. I turn in circles staring into the blurred sky, little burning cold flakes shooting straight down into my eyes.

•

Spring comes early. Sister Maria del Rey is preparing us for First Holy Communion, distributing holy cards to each of us. On one side is a picture of a young woman, startled from her reading by a dove. On the other side is a picture of Jesus.

The light coming in the windows of our first-grade classroom takes on a dark greenish cast. The sky brightens a moment and then explodes with a crack and a boom, but no rain falls.

Sister Maria del Rey explains that the young woman is the Virgin Mary and the dove is the Holy Ghost. "All three members of the Trinity are present in the Host that you will receive through this sacrament."

She lets us gather at the window and look out. When the clouds shatter and it pours, Communion takes on an aura of danger.

•

As I approach the communal kitchen at the youth hostel, I hear sounds: a cabinet opens, a drawer closes. I am nervous that when I look in, no one will be there. But there is someone. A young woman with blonde, curly hair, standing near the oven, turns and smiles at me. I nod at her, take a plate out of a cabinet, and put my packet of Ryvita crackers on it. She eyes them and offers me a grilled cheese and tomato sandwich, one of two she's just slid from a cast-iron frying pan onto a plate.

"Please! Please! Please!" she says in a halting accent, then puts the sandwich on a separate plate and holds it before me. She points at my jar of instant coffee, shakes her head, and points to a coffee pot percolating on the stove. She turns the burner off and pours us each a cup.

It is around four in the afternoon, and we sit together eating in the bright, empty dining hall, everyone else still off visiting the sites. I know no German but learn that her name is Brigitte. Her English is poor so I try speaking in

Spanish, but she shrugs apologetically. I wonder why all the other Germans I've met so far are fluent in English and she isn't. I have some sense that she does not quite fit with everyone else, but I am not able to put my finger on why.

Her clothes, very simple and clean, are worn. And facing her across the table I can see, by tiny lines around her eyes and at the corners of her mouth, that she is older than I thought, maybe in her early thirties. I notice she wears a wedding ring.

She has been in Killarney for two days, she tells me in broken English. I try to focus but I hear a buzz at the back of my head and see a shadow fall across the table. She senses something is wrong with me and reaches across the table, touching my forearm with her fingertips. Not knowing what else to do I point to my temple, feigning a headache.

•

My mother is yelling at my father, things I've heard Nanny say. "You are incapable of supporting this family. You are a dreamer and what good is that to any of us?" I sit at the table. I try not to listen. I watch the snow through a small opening in the curtain, and am anxious to go back out into it.

No one eats. With glazed eyes, Jerry gets up and runs from the room.

Crying, Tracy stands up and tries to follow him, but Mom won't let her.

"Sit down!" Mom demands, then goes into their bedroom and comes back with the big pale blue envelope in which she keeps love letters my father sent her when he was stationed in Korea during the war. "These are all a joke! You read through any of them and have yourself a big laugh."

She pours the letters out of the envelope and into the garbage, then empties her dinner plate, uneaten chicken and mashed potatoes, on top of the letters. My father jumps up to fish out the letters, cursing under his breath. All three of us girls start to cry, and now, when we get up to rush from the room, she doesn't stop us.

•

Brigitte and I ride in a horse-drawn wagon, what the locals call a pony-and-trap, through the Gap of Dunloe, a valley formed millions of years before by glacial ice. Cars are banned from the gap, but we see people wending their way by foot. The massive glacial rocks create strange echoes.

"Give a shout!" the driver recommends.

"Brigitte!" I yell and my voice echoes back at us.

She waits for the last audible echo to fade, then yells out, "Regina!"

I yell, "*Verfallenheit!*" and she yells, "Cornucopia!"

I tell her a word in English, and she shouts: *pamphlet, sandwich, shoes*. And she gives me German words to shout: *Bleinstift, Pferd, das Karminrot.* Each shout makes us laugh louder than the last.

After we ascend to a summit, a magnificent view between Macgillycuddy's Reeks and the Purple Mountains, the driver turns and says in a droll voice, "There's a pub up ahead but I don't think the two of you are in need of any libation."

Brigitte looks to me for translation. I point at the driver, then circle a finger a few times at my temple to indicate *crazy*, and then point at the two of us. We dissolve into laughter.

•

Nanny babysits us while my parents attend a PTA meeting. The others are all asleep when Nanny appears in the doorway to check on me. I pretend to sleep. A few minutes later I hear her in my parents' room and my stomach feels uneasy. I get up and peek out my door. I'm not sure what I am seeing. Nanny is naked, her pale body soft and sagging. She utters angry words in such a low register that I can't hear what they are. She slowly paces, arms swinging. She walks down the hall and into the living room, then circles around into the kitchen and out again into the bathroom. She seems to be going deliberately into each room but not to get anything or do anything, just muttering as she passes in and out of it naked.

•

I walk Brigitte to the bus station. She seems anxious. Passing a small church, she touches my arm and gestures that she wants to go in.

Inside is cool and dark. An old woman in a black shawl kneels at a pew near the front, saying the rosary, the click of beads and her whispers just audible in the silence. To the right of the altar, a black iron grid holds dozens of candles in votive glasses, several of them lit, a shimmer of pulsing flames. A small sign on the wall reads *Votives for the living, 5 pence. Votives for the dead, 10 pence.*

Brigitte watches as I take a match from a niche, light it on an existing flame, and whisper "Tracy" as I touch it to a new wick. I look at Brigitte and whisper the words she taught me: "*Mein Schwester.*" The flame is small, blue, and low at first, but in a moment rouses itself tall and emits a ribbon of smoke. When it settles into itself, I light one for Sheila and one for Jerry, each time saying their names, then slide three five-pence pieces into the offering slot.

•

I look at an old-fashioned picture of a girl dressed for Holy Communion in a scalloped lace veil, silky white dress, white stockings, and white shoes. Her ankles are thin but she is plump about the middle, an unhappy contraction around the lips. It is a misty image, more silvery than black-and-white. In the background, an alcove in a chapel, filled with lilies.

I stare into the girl's eyes, which stare back into mine.

"This is not you," I blurt out.

My mother laughs. "It *is* me," she says.

•

Brigitte lights two candles, whispering a name for each one. "Reiner. Ada." She then counts her coins, and puts what I think is probably too many into the slot.

A few minutes pass in meditation and when I touch her arm, gesturing that we should go, she recoils. Her eyes are filled with tears, her mouth set and trembling.

I look back at the flames and we remain, with only the sounds of the old woman's whispered sighs and clicking beads.

Before Brigitte gets on the bus, I ask, "Who are Reiner and Ada?"

She peers into my eyes. "Dead," she says. "My ... dead."

I point to her wedding ring. "Your husband? Dead?"

She tightens her mouth and shakes her head no. The door opens and she boards the bus. She waves from the window as the bus rounds the corner and disappears.

•

My mother kisses me on the temple on her way into the kitchen to make dinner. I stand in the doorway and watch her taking out pots and pans, opening cans and chopping lettuce as my sisters sit at the table coloring. When steam rises from the pot as it boils, I watch her put down a spoon, cross her arms, and stare out the window into the backyard.

·

The picture of beloved Uncle Michael is in my mother's nightstand drawer with a novena and a handkerchief embroidered with tiny purple flowers.

It is a formal pose, the way he stands holding his hat, eyes fixed to the camera, expression intent and thoughtful. My mother was his favorite.

·

I am home sick from school. My mother and father left for work and Nanny is in charge. Tracy and Sheila, still too young for school, are home also. I sleep the first hours of the morning away and awaken later with a pounding head. I wonder if there are two Nannies. Will the naked Nanny appear in my room while the other one is in the living room?

I get out of bed and find her in the living room with the curtain closed on the window, ironing and watching a movie on television. Afraid she will send me back to bed, I stay in the hallway, watching a commercial for Alka-Seltzer, a cartoon cutout of a smiling stomach dancing across the screen.

At the ironing board, Nanny mutters under her breath: "Goddamn son of a bitch piece of shit." This time I hear every word. She is focused on one of my father's shirts, which lies open before her, its sleeves hanging. Bringing the iron down hard on it, she holds it there and then spits onto the shirt, mumbles something, and picks up the iron, holding it high a moment before pounding it down again. She looks calm as she holds it there, her jaw set forward. When smoke and a burned smell rise up from the iron, I rush into the room. Startled, she gasps, and her jaw moves back and seems to disappear into the soft folds of her neck. Her eyes narrow and she looks worried and ashamed, as if she is not the same person she was a few seconds before.

"Get back to bed," she urges. "You're sick."

She walks in front of the ironing board, trying to hide the burned shirt, and before I can get out of the way I vomit on the floor, some of it spattering Nanny's calves and feet.

As I scream for my mother, Nanny cleans me and gives me ginger ale, then lets me come back into the living room and lie down on the couch. I stare on and off at the television.

•

The day after Brigitte is gone, I start asking around at the hostel if anyone is traveling north to Yeats country. Someone mentions that the two New Zealanders might be. I am aware of this couple. At dinner yesterday evening, I watched the uneasy dynamic between them: gray-eyed Ian, dark-haired and handsome, clearly smitten with petite, blonde, very fickle Caroline. One moment she snuggles up to Ian, and the next she's pushing him angrily away.

I approach them and ask if I might hitchhike with them to Yeats country.

Caroline's eyes brighten. "Yes!" she cries. Her excitement feels over the top, while Ian looks cross and says nothing.

But first, Caroline tells me, they are going south for a quick tour of the Ring of Kerry, which encircles the Iveragh Peninsula.

When I hesitate, Caroline persuades me to join them. I suspect that she wants me there as a kind of buffer between her and Ian. "We'll travel with you to Yeats country, but you can't leave this area without seeing the Ring of Kerry!"

·

I know the risk in telling my mother things I have seen. Even though she might start talking about dying and being a soldier, and she might scream and yell so Tracy and Sheila will hide in the linen cabinet and Jerry will have to go out and run in circles, pretending to shoot an invisible enemy with a machine gun, I need to tell her, and say in a calm, resigned voice, "Nanny burned Daddy's shirt with the iron."

Nanny purses her lips. "It was an accident."

"No, it wasn't," I say. "She spit at it and said bad words, and then burned it on purpose."

My mother remains quiet, her expression in the shadow difficult to read.

"Sometimes the iron is too hot and it burns things. Besides, you were sick. You don't remember what really happened," Nanny says.

"Yes, I do," I say.

Nanny pauses, then clucks her tongue, mutters something. She stands up and leaves the room.

"One night when you and Daddy weren't here, I saw Nanny walking around without any clothes on, going in all the rooms."

My mother peers into my face, her forehead furrowing. She looks like she wants to ask something but waits a while, then says, "Do you know what she was doing?"

"Spreading her molecules all over the house," I say.

•

Nanny has gone to the East to live with Uncle Jack and his wife. But even though she is gone, she has spread her molecules throughout the house, and most of them are in her room. No matter how much my mother airs out her room, there are still so many molecules in there, I can imagine them forming another Nanny.

I rush past Nanny's old room when I walk in the hall, afraid that if I look, I'll see her naked, holding a cigarette and exhaling smoke.

•

With Nanny gone, we travel to a national park or an Indian pueblo almost every weekend.

Mom buys a new white bedspread for her and Dad. *Candlewick*, she calls it, a kind of chenille, with clusters of raised threads that look like the wicks of candles. In the evening, the white bedspread gives off its own light.

•

We hike a trail along a lake, from Killarney to the hilltop town of Killorglin, the land green and lush, cows grazing among rocks and ruined walls, over which nettles, foxglove, and blackberry vines grow in profusion.

Killorglin, a beautiful, compact little town with colorful houses, is flanked on either side by lakes. The bed-and-breakfast Ian finds is on a narrow, steeply ascending street.

"Let's say we're married," Ian says, touching Caroline's arm.

She pulls away. "We don't *have* to do that!" Caroline says. "I'm sure they'll give us our own room, and Regina hers."

We knock and the landlady, a matronly figure with mild hazel eyes, ushers us into a small, bare foyer with blue floral wallpaper. I speak up first, asking for a single room. When Ian asks for a double, the landlady, seeing no ring on Caroline's finger, sets her mouth.

We follow her up a narrow carpeted staircase. "You two," she says to Caroline and me. "This is your room."

She looks at Ian, then says, "We're putting you downstairs."

•

On Mother's Day Dad gets the idea to go to the shelter and adopt a cat to give to Mom. He says that Susie won't like it at first but that she will learn to accept the cat.

We want a kitten, but Dad says it's better to rescue an older cat. We choose a male orange tabby. Mom names him Happy, short for Happy Mother's Day. Mom sits with him on the couch, petting him, and he purrs like a motor, gazing up at her.

"He's in love with you," Sheila says, and we all laugh because it seems true.

"I think he knows he's been rescued," Tracy says.

Mom calls him a sweet boy and he stands on her lap with his paws on her shoulders, rubbing his face against her chin, the rumble of his purr steady and loud.

"What a sweet boy!" Mom keeps saying, her face lit, her eyes half-closed.

•

For Father's Day, Mom buys Dad a chair, a big dark green comfortable chair that swivels. It sits in the center of the den facing the television, a place of honor.

·

In a beautiful little town called Sneem, on a green on the estuary of the Ardsheelhane River, I walk away from Caroline and Ian, who are embroiled in a nasty fight. I'm tired of the two of them.

It begins to rain. These storms that break and pass in minutes, that I no longer cover my head against, feel like a part of me now.

·

I am on the way back to my desk at school when I am stopped in my tracks by an image in a classmate's open book. At first I think it must be a picture of a sea creature, a shrimp or a sea horse, a frail network of veins visible under its translucent skin. It seems to float suspended though it is connected to a looping cord that rises up out of the frame of the picture, like the submerged stem of a lily pad. The creature is lit but hangs in darkness, small bright flecks around it. I take a step closer and my stomach clenches. There is something vaguely human about its overblown head and tiny praying hands.

"What is that?" I ask the girl who's looking at it.

"It's a baby in its mother's stomach."

"How did they take this picture?" I whisper.

"I don't know." She shrugs.

Another girl walks to the table, glances at it, and giggles.

Why are they not stunned?

I bend forward to study it more closely. An odor rises from the page, probably produced by the ink and the shiny treated paper, but there is another smell that seems more human mixed into it, like sweat.

·

Mom and Dad sit together on the edge of the white bed with the candlewick cover. They wear the same soft smile.

·

It is snowing. While I search for my gloves, the phone rings and somehow I know that it is Nanny. My mother, father, and siblings are already outside in the snow. I pick up the receiver and say, "Hello."

"Who's this?" Nanny yells. "Reggie? Tracy?"

I hesitate. "Reggie."

"What? I can't hear you. Let me talk to your mother," she demands.

I hesitate.

"Reggie! Can you hear me? Go get your mother!"

I put the receiver down on the table and go toward the front door, but don't open it. Instead, I go to the window and look outside. While my father scrapes the car windows, my mother, wearing her black hat and thick red coat, kneels with my brother and sisters, pushing a big wall of snow into a shape.

Soon, I hear Nanny's voice yelling from inside the receiver, strained and high-pitched. I start to laugh in an uncomfortable way that feels like a nervous contraction of the stomach muscles. Nanny screams, "Get your mother!" as if she can see me standing there, defying her. I walk to the phone and softly hang it up. I rush outside, where I fall to my knees next to my mother and start gathering snow. I imagine the phone ringing and ringing inside, where there is no one to hear it.

·

Tracy and I kneel on the couch pressing our faces to the cold window, watching cars pass, their windows fogged and frosted. We imagine that no one is driving them.

School has been canceled, and my mother and father stay home from work. I see them sitting on the edge of their bed with their arms around each other, not speaking, their eyes closed. They're unaware of me standing there watching them through the doorway. I don't feel as if I can enter. I cannot say what I sense in that embrace that makes me feel sad.

·

Nanny has been gone for more than a year and Mom asks Dad if she can come back and live with us. Dad agrees.

•

The whole family used to go to church together every Sunday. But after Nanny's back she never comes, and Mom stops coming, too, leaving it to Dad to take us. Dad drops us off most of the time, then picks us up afterward, his face flushed, his eyes damp and glistening. He instructs us not to tell Mom that he didn't attend. A few Sundays we have to wait for him in the empty parking lot after all the other parishioners have driven home.

•

"I want the least expensive coffin," Mom says. "And girls, I want you to scour the Salvation Army, and the Goodwill, even the Saint Vincent de Paul Society, for a military jacket."

"Barbara, for God's sake," my father pleads with her, but this makes her angrier.

"For God's sake is right," she yells. "I want a goddamn military jacket, and it doesn't even have to fit."

•

After leaving Caroline and Ian, I walk into the town and spot two bicycles with Killarney stickers leaning against a wall outside a restaurant. Inside it's quaint, brick walls

and hanging lamps. Two Welsh girls are the only customers. They tell me I shouldn't leave the area without seeing
Valentia Island, that I should go to Caherciveen a few
miles to the west and wait for the ferry across.

"There's going to be a fair there tonight," a waitress
who overhears us talking says. "And there's a hostel on
the island where you can stay." The Welsh girls are meeting someone in Killarney and have to leave soon, but I
consider going. The waitress says that if I wait an hour she
will give me a ride.

•

It is overcast and threatening rain. I walk down the length
of the pier, where I lean my heavy backpack against a stack
of empty wooden crates. A white boat is docked, rocking
on the waves. The name *Johnny Ruth* is painted in red script
on its side. I peer through gray mist at the island across the
bay. An hour or more goes by, a light rain sweeping in.

The figures of two men approach from the road. As
they get closer I see that they are both about my age.
One of them, with longish light brown hair and a jaunty
bounce to his step, calls out to me, "Waiting on the ferry,
are you?"

They are Irish—James and Denis.

I nod. "Yes. I've been here a long time."

"It might be a while still. It'll not come until the sky is
clearer," James says. "American, are you?"

"Yes."

Denis is wearing a red sweatshirt. He is tall and strong-looking with wavy dark auburn hair, cut shorter than his friend's. He says nothing and he doesn't smile.

•

When Nanny returns to live with us, she is gaunt, much older-looking. I'm not afraid of her in the same way.

She stops bothering to comb her gray tufts of hair, which have taken on a grizzled quality. She still covers her face with Noxzema at night, but no longer uses her compact and lipstick and relegates the jewelry she never wears to her top dresser drawer.

The first day she is back, Nanny sits in Dad's green swiveling chair in the den. After a few hours it is clear that she has claimed it and it no longer belongs to my father. Her hearing is worse than it was and she spends almost all her time in the chair with the television on loud, chain-smoking, the room shrill with commercial jingles and peals of canned laughter. The kitchen and the dining area are open to the den, and Nanny can swivel around any time she wants and survey what's happening.

The living room, across the hall, is a quiet refuge in comparison, separate from Nanny and the noise of the den. Mom likes to sit in there alone in her brown chair, drinking coffee or making lists.

•

The ritual of Nanny's pills becomes a big, nightly production. They have to be lined up in three Dixie cups and brought in to her on a tray. "The pills, Ba'bra. The pills," Nanny calls from her bedroom as she waits for them.

Mom has bought gelatin capsules and Tracy and I are enlisted once a week to fill lots of them with powdered milk in my mother and father's bathroom. Nanny gets four of these, two nervine capsules, and two aspirin. Tracy and I like the sneakiness of all of this.

"Pills for the pill," we say and laugh.

"Fixing pills for the giant pill."

•

"Seventy-six years old!" Nanny cries.

"Seventy-six trombones!" Mom echoes.

Tracy and I laugh hard at this and repeat it with Mom's inflection.

•

Long before any of us can see or even hear Dad's brown Chevy coming, our new puppy, Rory, knows and starts panting and whining. He's only three months old but he's already bigger than Susie, and stands on his hind legs, paws pressed to the screen door, barking, tail wagging out of control. He has a particular affection for Dad.

Poor Susie finds him irritating, but puts up with him. None of us can resist Rory. We all want to play with him, pet and tickle him and throw things for him to run after.

"Pet Susie!" Mom keeps saying. "Don't forget Susie!"

•

James and Denis cross with me to Valentia Island for the fair. The ferry, a small boat low to the water, tears at a slant across the surface of choppy waves. Denis sits staring down into the breaking water without seeming to see it. He glances at me when he feels me looking and I avert my eyes.

Once we dock, we go to a pub and I sit and watch Denis throw darts. James has drifted off to mingle with others at the bar. Denis throws a dart and hits near the bull's-eye and I clap. He looks at me smiling with surprise and hands me three darts. I throw them, not even hitting the board. We laugh and he buys us another round. I try Smithwick's, which he drinks, a dark red ale. Denis takes off his red sweatshirt and is wearing a worn beige Aran sweater. He's from Ballyferriter on the Dingle Peninsula, he tells me, speaking in a low register, mumbling as if he is eating his words.

"I was there," I say. "I think it's the most beautiful place in Ireland. Clogherhead Beach. The Three Sisters. Sybil Head."

He nods, his expression both shy and pleased.

I ask about a cottage I saw in the distance on a hill visible from Clogherhead Beach.

"Yes, I know the place."

"You do?" I ask, astonished.

"It's empty."

"Is it in shambles?"

"Maybe a bit. An itinerant woman lived there for a year or two. No one's there now but the spiders and the birds."

"I'd like to move into that cottage so I could always be near those beaches."

He looks at me sidelong with a little smile. "If I go back and I see a fire lit there at night, I'll come and check on you."

•

When it is almost dark we leave the pub and he reaches for my hand and holds it as we make our way to the Dairbhre Fair, where, in case the weather turns, the dancing is being held in a big barn crowded with locals and others who have crossed from the mainland for the festivities. The floor is covered in hay, the lighting dim with storm lanterns hanging on the walls.

A teenage boy in charge of the music changes the records on a rickety-looking Victrola in the corner. He has a limited choice of forty-fives and keeps playing Roxy Music's "Dance Away the Heartache." Everyone hooks arms with their partner and twirls around. Denis and I twirl each other fast, gaining a thrilling momentum, so the force throws us a little each time we let go of the other's arm. Rapt and dizzy, we try to catch our breath, eyes damp with laughter.

•

Mom leads us outside to the backyard after it has rained and tells me to stand near the slender apple sapling and breathe.

"What do you smell?" she asks.

Though it has produced no fruit yet, after the rain, the young tree smells of apples.

•

My father brings Nanny home a carton of Salems and presents it to her with a flourish. "Here you are, Mrs. Tully," he says.

Taken aback, she thanks him.

"You are very welcome," he says.

As soon as he turns, she mutters, "Stupid piece of shit."

He freezes a moment, then continues to move away.

Tracy and I have witnessed this and begin our secret campaign against Nanny. We lie under our beds and write with pencil on the bed boards: *I hate Nanny. Nanny stinks. Nanny will go to hell.*

•

Among all my mother's unsorted photographs, there is a studio picture of Nanny and my grandfather, with my uncle Jack, a year old, looking startled and bemused, sitting on Nanny's lap. Fleshy in a pale chiffon dress, her brown hair carefully arranged, Nanny wears an imperial expression on her face. My grandfather, who looks like a tall James Cagney, stares off to the side as if he is far away in his thoughts.

•

For days before we leave for a vacation to the Grand Canyon, Nanny yells at Mom.

"Let Vincent take the kids! It's selfish of you to leave me here."

She throws her dinner on the floor, complains the coffee's cold and spills it. She holds a lit cigarette to the arm of the swiveling chair.

Mom has hired a woman named Mrs. Janney to stay with Nanny the four days we will be gone. Mom's stocked the kitchen with Nanny's favorite foods: cans of chicken a la king, chocolate cream pies.

The morning we are leaving, as Dad backs the car out of the driveway, Mrs. Janney comes out and calls Mom in.

Ten minutes pass before Mom comes out again. She's agitated and slams the car door. "Let's go, goddammit!" she yells at my father.

•

It is a clear night full of stars, the clouds having moved far off into the Atlantic. The cool island air still smells of rain from earlier in the day. As Denis and I walk, holding hands, I tell him I am moving to Dublin, that I want to have a life as an actress. I tell him that in Santa Fe I played Cassandra, the prophetess, in *The Trojan Women*, and made my entrance each night onto a dark stage holding a lit torch. I describe the feeling of looking out, the audience in darkness so I could not see them, nor could I see the walls of the theater itself, so it was as if the entire night sky were open before me. And how as I stood there and lifted my head and spoke a monologue, a prayer to the god Apollo, there was intense silence because everything spoken from the stage seems to mean more. I tell him that I will never forget the feeling of speaking out into that darkness and feeling it listen.

He takes my hand and holds it and looks into my face with a spark of curiosity. He seems moved by what I've told him. "You'll get the job in the theater in Dublin," he says. "I'm sure of it."

It's sweet the way he phrases it, as if there's something permanent about a role in a play.

Walking along the shore we arrive at a bench, and sit facing the mainland. He kisses me and, after a few moments, with a shaking breath, breaks the kiss. I rest the side of my face against his collarbone, his heart beating against my neck, quick and hard.

If he hadn't broken the kiss, I would not have.

Still embracing me, he says, "Tell me more about standing on the stage, looking out into the darkness."

I breathe in his scent and it is familiar to me: like stones in the rain. Though we met only hours ago, we know each other.

"I felt my parents there, watching me."

He waits for me to go on.

"They died."

I breathe him in again.

"How?"

"I can't tell you," I say, though I have a strong desire to tell him. I want to deepen what's between us.

I stay quiet and he peers into my eyes, a shadow forming on his brow. "You can. You can tell me."

Around us the Irish air, Irish darkness over Irish ocean.

"You won't want to kiss me anymore if I tell you."

"I will still want to kiss you."

After a silence I take the risk. "They killed themselves."

He blinks, waits a moment, then says, "That's not your fault."

"But they were my parents."

He shakes his head. "But they aren't you."

He tightens his grip on my hand. I look into his face, then sigh and go quiet. He leans close and kisses me.

"You see? I still want to kiss you."

A bell rings at the hostel to announce the impending curfew. We walk toward the light that shines over the hostel door, but Denis stops and embraces me while we are still in the shadows. I say to him, "If I ever move into that little house facing Clogherhead Beach, and you see firelight there at night, you'll come, won't you, and check on me?"

He brings his face very close to mine so our foreheads are touching, then says something in Irish.

"What did you say?" I ask, our foreheads still pressed close.

"I said if I ever see firelight in that little house, I'll come up and check on you."

Because of the fair, the ferries are running late into the night. He has to go back to the *Johnny Ruth*, but promises to return the next evening. We step into the porch light, holding hands. Just before parting I ask him to speak to me again in Irish. I close my eyes, letting the soft sounds splash over me.

•

Mom talks about being a soldier.

My sisters and brother stare out at the passing desert. We have been driving for hours, but we're not even halfway to the Grand Canyon.

"And when I die, I want a crew cut," Mom says.

In the rearview mirror Dad's mouth looks tight. I watch the moving lines of the highway reflect on his sunglasses.

Sheila whispers something into the bright blonde hair of the doll she clutches to her chest.

•

We go horseback riding at the southern rim of the Grand Canyon. As she has said she would, Mom asks for a spirited horse. Now and then on the trail, Mom takes her horse ahead in a wild gallop. After a few miles, the horse I am on decides it is sick of a slow saunter and bolts. I grasp the reins, the horn, and the saddle. The galloping bumps me up and down, hurls me loose. The hooves pounding against rocky earth send blows through my body until I am sliding sideways off the horse. Through a deafening whistle of wind, I hear Mom scream, "Hold on. Hold on." And then she is there, her horse galloping alongside mine. She leans into me and grasps me with one arm. I don't know how she manages to do it, but she gets me off the bolting horse and onto hers.

When we arrive back at the stables, I am still shaking so violently I can't stand. The astounded trail guides compliment my mother. No one mentions the fact that at eleven, I am almost as tall as she is, and probably weigh the same.

After rescuing me she seems restored, rejuvenated. Everything after that feels heightened, as if we are breathing extra oxygen.

•

It's a hot July day and the four of us kids have been swimming and playing for hours in the motel pool, which we've had virtually to ourselves. Jerry throws an army man into the deep end at the six-foot mark. I gulp in a big breath, then go under, my feet splashing as I descend. The soldier is in a standing position, drifting about an inch above the pool floor, and I am able to snatch it. I surface, my arm raised, clutching my prize.

When I get out of the pool there are chlorine haloes around everything: the big umbrella, the towel, and the tube of Coppertone. Tracy walks, waist-deep, in the shallow end with Sheila on her shoulders. The aqua pool water shimmers around them like a million particles of light.

•

The weather is clear, but I am anxious for the hours to pass until I see Denis again. I rent a bike and ride around the island, and I stop at a big gray house, in an area called Ballyhearney. There is a plaque on it that says it was once a famine hospital. I try the door, but it is locked. I walk in a circle around it. I can see inside the smudged windows a spooky emptiness. In one otherwise bare room, a narrow iron headboard leans against a wall.

I ride the bicycle up a dirt hill and stop when I come to an overgrown field where a white horse stands grazing.

•

We are driving past acres of dry fields when Mom spots a big black horse standing at a fence and asks Dad to pull over.

"He's a giant!" Dad says.

Us kids crowd Mom as she gets an apple out of a bag in the trunk. "You have to hold your hand out flat like this, then the horse won't nip your fingers by mistake."

Just as we're approaching the fence where the horse is waiting, a lady in a cowboy hat and jeans appears, coming out of a stable. She pulls a hose that runs with water, and puts it into a trough to fill it. She nods at us and says it's okay to give the horse an apple.

"What's his name?" Mom asks.

"Angus," she answers.

Mom and Dad look at each other, smiling and surprised.

"Who is Angus?" I ask.

"It's a name out of Irish myth," Dad says.

Angus laps the apple off Mom's hand. While he crunches it, juice spilling from between his teeth, the lady says, "He's gentleness itself!"

Mom strokes his neck, then leans in and kisses the side of his face.

At home I look in the book of Irish myths and read that Angus is the Irish god of love.

•

As evening sets in, I gravitate toward the pier, my heart pounding as a ferry comes in. The closer it gets, the clearer it is that Denis is not on it. I sit down on the bench where I sat with Denis the night before. The ferry leaves and returns a little later, but again Denis isn't on it.

"Je reviens," I whisper, eyes set on the ferry's path across the water.

Maybe he has thought about how my parents died and finds it too terrible. I read in an old book about the British Isles that the Irish drove stakes into the hearts of suicides.

The night passes and Denis never comes.

∙

From behind our half-open door, Tracy and I spy on Nanny as she walks down the hall in the middle of the day and stops outside the bathroom. Instead of going in and closing the door, she opens her legs to a wide stance and waits, then strains and pushes, grunting. A few moments later she calls, "Ba'bra. Ba'bra."

∙

In our closet behind the dresses and coats, Tracy and I write all over the walls in pen: *I hate Nanny. Nanny stinks. Fuck Nanny. I want Nanny to die and go to hell.*

We wrack our brains to come up with some trick we can play on Nanny, some way to scare her.

•

"Uncle Michael loved my mother," I say to Nanny.

I notice the slight acceleration in the rise and fall of her sunken chest.

"My mother was his favorite."

She glares at me through the filthy lenses of her glasses.

•

Dad is working and Mom is at a PTA meeting. Nanny and Sheila are watching Liberace play a rhinestone piano on the *Lawrence Welk Show*. Tracy and I try to interrupt Nanny's enjoyment by mocking his nasal voice: "I love the *pyano*. I love the *pyano*."

Nanny waves her arm at us. "Sssshhh!" she says.

It isn't enough. We want to do something more.

The fuse box for the entire house is in our room. I switch off the power, and, in sudden darkness, Liberace goes quiet midmeasure. From the doorway of the den, where Tracy has been waiting, holding a big powder puff loaded with dusting powder, she rushes into the dark and feels for Nanny's face, then slaps her with the powder puff, all the while Nanny and Sheila are screaming.

When we switch the power back on and go in and look at them, Sheila is clinging to Nanny, whose face is white with powder. Nanny blinks, opening and closing her mouth, trying to push the powder out with her tongue. Sheila has powder all over the top of her hair and on her dress. I start to laugh, though my stomach spasms with remorse.

"I hate you guys," Sheila says. She's crying.

•

The trees have grown high all around the house.

"A grove," Mom says. "We're living in a grove."

•

I have thought of staying an extra day on Valentia Island but the idea of waiting another agonizing night for Denis and him never coming is not bearable.

I find two Americans, Philip and Jan, to hitchhike north with.

While we are on the ferry back to Cahirciveen, I see the *Johnny Ruth* docked there, Denis on the pier bent over a mass of heavy wet rope, organizing it into a damp coil. He stands the last few minutes, watching and waiting for the boat to come in, and when it aligns itself with the pier, he reaches in and helps me climb out.

Philip and Jan drift off ahead and wait for me a few yards away.

"You didn't come last night," I say, struggling to keep my mouth from trembling.

"I'm sorry," he says. "We had to go out with the nets." They just got back an hour ago, having gotten no sleep the night before.

He told me the night on Valentia that a fisherman is dependent on weather and the mood of the water, that conditions all around the western coast of Ireland are rocky and dangerous, that sometimes they're forced to wait a week before they can fish. When the weather is with them, they have to go out.

James appears and catcalls from the deck of the boat. Denis waves his hand dismissively at him.

I want to press my face against his neck, smell his skin and his Aran sweater. But we are in the daylight and there are other people around us.

He glances over toward Philip and Jan.

"Some Americans also traveling north," I say.

"I'm coming to see Dublin," Denis says.

"When?"

"Three weeks, when we're finished here."

I give him Theresa's address and phone number. "I may be there," I say, "but if not, she'll know where I am."

I watch as he writes his parents' Ballyferriter address and phone number in my address book and hands it back to me.

"I wrote it in Irish," he says.

•

In Limerick we stop at a pub for lunch. After eating, Jan spreads her map out on the table before us. Yeats country is about six hours to the north. They suggest we stop two hours to the northwest in Doolin or Lisdoonvarna, where the best Irish music in the world is played in the pubs. Though I'm feeling a little anxious to get to Yeats country, I want to hear the music. And I don't want to lose them as my traveling companions. Before we go, though, they express interest in looking around the town of Limerick, so I tell them to leave their packs with me at the pub and I'll guard them. I'm feeling sad about Denis, and wouldn't mind an hour or so alone.

There's a man staring at me from the bar, a rugged-looking character, heavyset with shaggy black hair. After a few minutes he approaches and hands me a weighty metal plaque, around five inches by five inches, with the words *God Bless Our Home* engraved into it.

"For you," he says.

Taken aback, I thank him.

"I made this," he says. "Forged it with my own two hands."

Turning it over, I see in small words at the bottom right corner: *Made in China*, and a registered trademark symbol stamped into it. I pretend not to see this. "Beautiful!"

He eyes the backpacks. "Are your friends coming back straightaway?"

"Yes, any minute now."

He gazes dreamily at me and says, "Sure, you must look lovely in nothing but your pelt."

I smile as if I don't know what this means, hold the plaque up, and say, "Thanks again!"

When he retreats, a woman who has been clearing glasses behind the bar approaches me and points to a sign on the wall with a painting of a bull on it and the words: *Beware of the Bull.* Then she tilts her head in the shaggy-haired man's direction.

PART FOUR

I clap and stomp my foot on the pub's worn wooden floor as a motley group of musicians play pipes, fiddle, bodhran, and flute, many of the jigs familiar: fast-paced, high-energy music full with joy. The two big, sweet guys who run Tommo's, the hostel down the road where I'm staying, nod their heads in time and smile bleary-eyed. The one with the black beard winks at me. In the mornings they cook and serve the breakfasts in aprons, overseeing everything with finicky attention, but by afternoon they've arrived here to the pub and parked themselves at the bar, drinking pints of Guinness, watching the comings and goings of the various girls staying in their establishment.

A woman stands up and sings along to a tune I know well: "The Black Velvet Band."

•

In a haze of wet light, I wander alone on winding roads outside of Doolin, looking at farmland and nearby ranges of mountains. A tall, fat goose guarding a field around a thatched cottage on the road to Liscannor waddles toward me as I near its property. I speak to it, trying to make friends, or reach some kind of understanding. It cranes its neck, stepping from foot to foot, then breaks into a chase. I run, laughing and breathless, until it stops and turns back, satisfied with my distance from its jurisdiction.

•

Philip and Jan leave for Yeats country on the second day in Doolin, but I remain behind. There is something welcoming and easy about this place, and something hypnotic about the music. Hours, entire days go by as I listen to long improvisational sessions weaving one piece into another, repetitions, variations, long traipsing fugues. Closing my eyes, I feel as if I'm swimming in the music. Time loses its coherence.

The fourth night at Tommo's on the edge of sleep, I think of Yeats country and imagine the sacred woods, the giant Irish deer. The images comfort me, but I make no move the next day to get there.

•

Two of the Swiss girls I've been going to the pub with have invited me to take the ferry across for a day trip to the Aran Islands. We will all meet at the pier for the one o'clock boat. An hour before, while the two of them are at the beach, I go to a small local shop.

It's all shadows at first when I walk in from the daylight, and for the flash of a moment, I mistake a side of dark, coppery-smelling bacon hanging from a hook for a person. I approach the counter where a stack of peat bricks for sale issues a black, earthy coolness. "Hello," I call out.

Silence. Under the foggy glass cover of a cake dish, a rope of pale sausages lies curled up in a pile.

I feel someone here. I don't move. After a beat, I hear fidgety squeaking from the back of the shop and a breathy, dejected groan. Whoever it is is listening for me to move.

I take a step and look down the last aisle. On a chair in the corner, a woman sits stiffly, her eyes cast off to the side. She appears to be in her thirties, though it is hard to know for certain. Her skin is dull yellow and pulls tight against sharp cheekbones. She lets out a sudden breath, as if bristling at my presence. I both pity and fear her. Then, leaning forward, she cocks her head slightly and looks at me. I see my mother, her square jaw and wet blue eyes. The air around me goes heavy as water and twinkles like flecks of glitter swirling in a snow globe. I make myself focus. The woman's nose and mouth and many other things about her face are nothing at all like my mother's.

Even still, she retains some element of my mother. I turn so I can no longer see her, and walk toward the door, which looks far away. The air in the place tries to hold me there, to keep me from moving, but I strain against it. Everything is too slow. With great effort I pass faded advertisements on the wall, a green cardboard one for Player's cigarettes, and a yellow picture of a cow that says *Yeats country*, and in smaller letters beneath, the word *dairy*. I hear footsteps as I retreat through the door, pushing my way outside into brightness.

•

Mom selects a white coffin, upholstered in blue silk quilting, and a pale blue silk-and-lace gown. She tells me that the morticians will wash and comb and style Nanny's hair, which has not been tended in years. They will put on lipstick and powder, and polish her nails. She asks me to go with her to pick out jewelry. "You're artistic," she says. "You'll know what to get."

We drive in silence to a store downtown. We pick out cameos: a necklace and a pin. She is worried that the ivory and pale beige colors won't go with the blue of the gown but I assure her that they will.

"I don't know," she says. "What do I know?"

•

Mom and Nanny sit at the kitchen table, drinking coffee and talking with great animation about people they knew in Yonkers.

"That woman would lie about anything and not bat an eye!" Nanny says.

"No one would ever suspect that!" Mom replies, shaking her head.

"She asked me once for a quarter to buy bread and potatoes for her kids. I saw her half an hour later at the drugstore drinking an ice cream soda!"

When Mom laughs, Nanny breaks a smile.

•

It is a rare overcast and windy morning. Mom has traveled back East with Nanny's coffin. My father and Jerry have put Nanny's green swiveling chair into the trunk of the car, leaving it open. We drive to the dump. When Dad and Jerry heave the chair onto the mountain of garbage, the cushion separates and flies at an arc, landing at a distance on the heap. The chair falls on its back at an angle facing the sky. Crows and carrion birds shriek and circle above.

My father lights a cigarette, shielding the flame from the wind with his cupped hand. When I first see the flame, I think it is meant for the chair.

"Can we throw a match at the chair?" I ask.

My father looks amused as he exhales a mouthful of smoke.

"This isn't a bonfire," he says.

It smells terrible here and the birds caw. Some sit on the garbage and stare at us. Everything here is destroyed, smashed, discarded. Even still, we all remain looking at the chair.

·

It is time to meet the Swiss girls at the pier, but after leaving the shop I am too shaken. I walk back in the direction of Tommo's. I don't want to believe it, but it is so real to me in this moment: my mother has been absorbed somehow by that unbalanced woman and is damned in her afterlife to remain part of her.

I have it in my head that I saw a rope tied around one of the woman's ankles, that she'd been restrained in the corner. And then I think that maybe she had no arms. I don't remember seeing any.

The road, the sky, even the stones on the ground look distorted and everything emits a high-pitched hum.

As I move quickly along the roadside, I hear a dry, uneven panting amplified over the sound of my own breathing and heartbeat. The woman is pursuing me, wanting me to look in her eyes again, so I'll see my mother stuck there, suffering in this awful, claustrophobic union.

Though Tommo's was my destination, I pass it, continuing down the road. In my pocket I have a rough map that one of the proprietors drew for me the day before, the walking directions to the Cliffs of Moher, a seven-mile trek there and back. I head in that direction.

•

When Mom comes back from the East, she opens the window in Nanny's room to air it, intending to clear things out, but retreats and stands there right outside the door staring at the mirror from an angle that doesn't reflect her, just the crucifix and the bare wall and the window full of daylight. I stand there, too, in the hall, a few feet behind her.

Before she left for the East she took some of Nanny's clothes out of the drawers, and now they lie in crumpled disarray, some folded, some on top of the dresser, some on the bed. A gust comes through the screen of the open window, making the clothes quiver. One faded old slip, lying precariously on the edge of the bed, blows to the floor. The door begins to creak closed, then slams shut of its own accord. Mom does not move from her spot, her face only inches from the slammed door. I touch her arm, wanting her to come away, but she remains there with a hurt, stunned expression on her face.

•

A perpetual soft, uneasy rustling comes from Nanny's room.

·

The following weekend, when Nanny's things still have not been cleared out, I am in the kitchen with my mother.

"Ba'bra! Ba'bra!" The voice comes from up the hall.

"For the love of God," my mother says, her face going white. She and I rush to the hall and for the flash of a moment, we see Nanny.

I grasp what we are seeing before my mother does. Sheila has put on one of Nanny's old dresses and sits on Tracy's shoulders. Tracy is hidden beneath the dress. They walk down the hall toward us, one awkward, slow-moving being.

When she understands, my mother's face empties of feeling. She doesn't get mad at them, but in a quiet voice tells them to take off the dress and never to do anything like it again.

She makes herself a cup of coffee and goes to sit alone in the living room.

·

On a hot summer day, Jerry teaches me to drive Dad's brown Chevy, coaching me as I reverse out of the drive-way. I steer slowly and shakily down the street, panicking when another car comes up and honks behind me.

"It's okay, Reg, they'll pass, don't worry." He sticks his arm out the passenger window and waves them on.

I head toward the rodeo grounds and pull onto a wide dirt road flanked by stretches of dry mesa. I drive in circles and experiment with going in reverse.

"You're really doing a great job," Jerry says. "You'll be an expert before you know it."

•

The higher I go on the pass to the summit, the harder the wind blows. I walk across an expanse of flat stone and stand looking at a progression of five cliffs, flat at the top with grassland and heath, and falling sheer to the sea, seven hundred feet at their highest point, I have been told. They are layered in sandstone and shale, patched in spots with green moss or lichen. Birds that nest in the shelves of rock, thousands of them, small as specks from where I stand, circle and screech below, all up and down the height of each cliff, their cries mournful, just audible over the low thunderous noise of the sea.

Why haven't I left Doolin already? I should be walking in hazel woods in Yeats country.

•

I have just turned fourteen. I stand in the dark front yard on a spring night, the wind going wild in my mother's trees. I am transforming, growing out of childhood, getting taller and slimmer, amazed by the slope between my waist and hips. I lift my head high and lean it back, my hair assaulted by the gusts. I hold my arms out away from my body, palms lifted, and think of the word *rapture*.

Sensing someone at the screen door, I drop my arms and turn. It's Dad looking out at me. I feel embarrassed, caught at something so personal, a private form of devotion. Dad steps outside from the low-lit vestibule and stands a few moments on the porch.

I wonder if he will ask what I was doing, and I am ready to shrug it away somehow, dismiss it. But he doesn't say anything for a little while, just stands looking at me. He seems tentative, as if he's afraid he's trespassed.

Then he recites:

> *Who has seen the wind?*
> *Neither I nor you:*
> *But when the leaves hang trembling*
> *The wind is passing thro'.*

He gets in the car and backs out of the driveway, headlights illuminating the houses as he turns onto Louraine Street and disappears.

The wind blows so hard in the poplars and the willow, it sounds like a waterfall.

•

At dinner, Dad tries to sprinkle salt over his rice, but nothing comes out.

"This is empty," he says.

"Oh, God help us!" Mom cries, getting up. "The *man* of the house has no salt!"

While we all sit unmoving and silent, she grabs the shaker and fills it, then slams it down before my father on the table.

"The *man* of the house!" she screams, prolonging the word *man*. "The *man* of the house needs salt!"

Dad, who has been still, reaches for the pot of peas and pours the contents over his head, wearing the pot like a hat. Peas spill over his shoulders and shirt, all over the floor.

For a few moments, Mom is silent. When she starts again to speak, Dad takes the pot off his head, stands, gets his jacket, and leaves an hour early for his shift at the Tap Room.

•

Jerry starts buying pot by the pound and selling lids from the window of his room. He keeps the pot hidden in his bumper pool table. I go to Jerry's room to ask him for a joint.

I find him sitting on his bed holding a shoe box full of rocks, the ones he's been collecting for years. He looks up from them, and says something that shocks me: "Mom's taken up Nanny's crusade against Dad. She hates Dad like Nanny hated Dad. Only worse."

•

When it's dark, Tracy and I take the joint Jerry gave us out to the aqua Dodge Dart, a used car Dad bought for Jerry to use. It's parked on the street beside the poplars. We listen to the radio and get high. No one can see us in the car in the dark, but we can see the people who step out of their houses onto their lit porches, or pass along the street. We rename our neighbors as they pass: Bobby Pringle becomes Blobby Pretzel. The twins Reid and Randy Warner become Weed and Pansy Foreigner. Ben Vigil becomes Bean Vengeance.

We laugh until our sides hurt and our eyes are wet.

•

Mom finally undertakes the emptying of Nanny's drawers and closet; she won't let any of us help. She often stops and sits on Nanny's sheetless bed. I watch her from the doorway as she holds one of Nanny's earrings in her hand, a clear light blue earring that looks like a small ice cube.

•

I wake to screaming and when I come out of my room, I see Mom on the hall floor. I run and try to help her get up. She grabs my ankle with such a strong grip that I almost fall.

"You can't pass," she growls in a voice slurred with rage and exhaustion. "You have to walk on me." I refuse and she tries again to grab my ankle.

Sheila appears in her pajamas, squinting from her bedroom door.

"Walk on me," Mom demands. Sheila, unsure what to do, attempts to walk across her back, then gets off, shaking and on the verge of tears.

When Jerry arrives at the end of the hall, Mom yells at him, "Put on your boots and walk on me." He disappears.

"Jerry," she screams. "Jerry."

I rush past Mom to the end of the hallway and look through the doorway into the kitchen and den that lead to Jerry's room. He stands frozen, head hanging, in the middle of the dark den, illuminated by a soft light through the open door of his room.

"Jerry," I say, "what should we do?"

His hunched shoulders stiffen at my voice, but he doesn't move. When I say his name again, I walk toward him and in a flurry of panic he rushes into his room. I hear the door lock.

Going back toward the hall, passing the dark kitchen, I wonder what time it is, but do not think to switch on the kitchen light and look. I both hope and fear that my father will arrive home from the Tap Room.

"Jerry," Mom cries out again. Twisting her head up from the floor, she says, "Tell Jerry to put on his boots."

"You have to stop it," I say. "You have to get up."

She lifts her head a little, straining her eyes upward to look at me as she sticks her tongue out and touches it to the floor.

"Mom, please stop," I plead, starting to cry. "Stop."

As I reach down and try to make her get up, she grabs my foot and bites it hard. I scream and struggle to get it away from her.

Maybe it's the sight of blood on my foot, or the taste of it in her mouth, that makes all the fight in her drain away.

•

My mother winds the white rosary around my hands, which are steepled together in prayer. She makes sure that the little crucifix faces front. She adjusts my Communion veil so it fountains evenly over both shoulders.

The photographer goes under a black tarp behind a big standing camera. As Mom moves off to the side, she nods approval. I am her beautiful bride. I smile at her as the shutter clicks.

•

We ask if we can take the car and go see the new version of *Wuthering Heights*. Mom agrees and gives us money.

Tracy, who really has expressed interest in seeing it, is easily persuaded not to when I tell her that Jerry has given me a joint. She says that she would rather smoke. "I'm nervous to see a movie version, anyway," she says. "I'm afraid they might ruin it." *Wuthering Heights* is Tracy's favorite book.

We sit on the car parked at an overlook in Tesuque, the radio on loud, the car doors open. The song "Ruby Tuesday" casts a reflective, melancholy spell on us.

Tracy lies back on the windshield, looking up at the stars. "I'll tell you what *Wuthering Heights* is about," she says.

"Mom probably won't even ask."

Tracy insists, and I listen as she summarizes the tumultuous and tragic story of Cathy and Heathcliff, up to the end when a shepherd boy sees the ghosts of the two of them near a tree on the moor.

"Why did things have to be so terrible between them?" I ask.

She doesn't answer, just keeps looking at the sky.

"Why doesn't Dad stop Mom?"

She is quiet and I worry that I shouldn't have asked it. Tracy gets angry with me sometimes for saying things. I don't always know what will make her mad, but she holds hard to a grudge, and I don't want to lose her. She doesn't look angry, so I take a chance and ask, "Why does Mom hate Dad so much?"

I think at first that she's ignoring the question when she says, "There's a scene where Cathy tells the maid, 'Nelly, I am Heathcliff!'"

But then her lips tremble and she closes her eyes. She adds, "'He's more myself than I am.'"

•

Dr. Brumlop, a large, fair-haired woman in her late fifties, listens as Mom chronicles my delinquent behavior.

Since Nanny died Mom's upsets are much more frequent and much worse. She has come one or two times to see Dr. Brumlop to get prescriptions of Seconal. It is meant to help her sleep when she has insomnia, but the Seconal does not help my mother sleep. It does not even relax her, but prolongs and intensifies the unhappy episodes, makes her bang into walls or fall, slurring her words and crossing her eyes. She does not need Seconal to get into a state, but it does nothing to help.

But we are here today to talk about me. Someone Mom works with saw me at a red light on Cerrillos Road at ten thirty on a school morning, in the passenger seat of a car. It was bad enough that I was supposed to be in school at that hour, but then I rolled down the window and, clearly drunk, puked all down the side of the car door.

I feel Dr. Brumlop's eyes on me as I stare through the big office window, which is slightly ajar, and focus on the soft gurgling of a fountain in a private garden, the statue of a gray Buddha meditating in a bed of marigolds.

Dr. Brumlop asks Mom to go into the waiting room so she can speak with me, and when we are alone she asks me vague questions about my behavior. For a moment I have no idea what I might say. I try to answer. It's just the way things are, I tell her. I hate the conventional world and have not an iota of interest in school. I want to live in the beauty of the moment.

Without really thinking about it, I find myself telling her how Mom tried to drink the Drano, and about a night when Mom told us that she'd taken a bottle of pills, and how my father called an ambulance. It turned out that she'd lied and when they pumped her stomach they found nothing. She blamed my father for it and said it was his fault she'd had to endure that. I ask Dr. Brumlop, "He was right, wasn't he, to call an ambulance?"

Dr. Brumlop's glasses, which sit low on her nose, reflect the light through the window and glint, obscuring her eyes, but her mouth has fallen open and her eyebrows are drawn together.

"Yes," she says, "he was right."

•

I sit on a rock wall at the Cliffs of Moher with a vast view of the sea below. Sometimes, though, I don't look at the sea at all, but down at the sneakers I'm wearing, a pair I bought in Killarney: black and white and bright orange. It's the orange I don't want to stop looking at, the way it emits a fierce glow in the overcast afternoon.

•

On the scribbled map he made me, the proprietor from Tommo's did a rough drawing of the cliffs. He drew an arrow pointing to the last cliff, which I can see from where I sit. Above the arrow, he wrote the words *Hag's Head*.

•

I am with two other girls in a car ditching school on a winter day. I am sixteen. We're laughing about something as we zoom along a bare stretch of desert highway, the air in the cab filled with pot smoke.

I spot my father walking, not dressed for the cold, wearing only a light jacket. He is not far from the Tap Room. My brother has told me that some nights my father sleeps in his car in the parking lot, so I imagine the car must still be parked there and not starting. If he ran the engine all night to keep the heat on, the battery has probably died.

I don't mention to my friends that I see him. It will take him an hour and a half to get home by foot and most of the distance he will have to travel will be along bare desert. There is no way we can pick him up and give him a ride. I am supposed to be in school and the car reeks of pot.

I watch as my father's figure recedes, growing tiny in the rearview mirror. I stare through the windshield at the empty stretch of land and watch the cold wind shake the piñon brush.

•

I wake from near sleep. Sheila, at two and a half, keeps getting out of bed and going in the hall, calling out to

Mommy. Since she stopped using a crib, she sleeps in a room with me and Tracy.

"Sssshhh, sweetie," Mom says, carrying her in again and covering her.

"'Molly Mone'!" Sheila whispers. She means the song "Molly Malone." "Sing 'Molly Mone'!"

In a voice just above a whisper, Mom sings:

> *She drove her wheelbarrow*
> *Through streets broad and narrow,*
> *Crying cockles and mussels, alive, alive oh!*

On Mom's voice, I float back to sleep.

•

The water hurls itself hard at the cliff and rises straight up into the air, twenty, maybe thirty feet before collapsing into foam. The gulls, riding the wind, are tuned to the sea's rhythms. Their screams, earnest, echoing pleas, intensify as the water stirs, hurling itself again at the rocks, and rising straight up into air.

"Hallo!" A voice from behind me in the distance disrupts my reverie. I'm still afraid to turn. It gets closer. "Hallo!" it repeats. It's a male voice with an accent. I twist around and look.

A guy about my age, wearing a bright yellow windbreaker, waves at me. He's smiling, a shock of light curly blond hair around his face. I wave back as he approaches. When he's a yard away, he takes out a crumpled map and points to one of the other cliffs where there is a stone tower.

"Did you . . . went? Go?" he asks, winded from climbing. I shake my head no.

He looks down at the view of the water, whistles with awe, then looks at me, his smile intensifying. "Ah!" he says, opening his arms, then turning to take in the view all around.

"I am Will," he says, pointing to himself.

"My name is Regina," I say. "I'm American."

"I am Dutch." He tells me he is from a place called Breda in Holland.

We speak to each other in phrases and single words, nodding and gesturing.

He points again at the other headland with the castle tower. The two of us set out together, taking a path that he finds on his map. When we see a cow behind a fence he asks me to take a picture of him with it. He sits on the fence reaching his hand out to the cow. When it makes a sudden groaning noise, the two of us look at each other and laugh. After this, everything makes us laugh, including a fat horse standing in high grass chewing and watching us, its ears alert. I drop the bag I'm carrying and things spill out and roll down the hill and he runs after them. A small bottle of lotion keeps rolling just as he almost has it and this makes us laugh even more.

I feel a smile now on my face as perpetual as the smile on his.

As we walk I ask if he is a student and he says no, that he works in a department store "selling . . . toys."

"Toys!" I cry, delighted. It seems so fitting.

"But not *all* toys! Only . . ." He is not sure how to say it. "*Soft* toys."

"Oh!" I say. "Do you mean stuffed toys?"

He seems uncertain if it's the right word.

"Like soft bears and rabbits?"

"Yes, yes. *Soft* toys."

We climb to each different cliff, and arrive at the last one, Hag's Head, which reaches farthest into the Atlantic. We photograph each other with the ancient gray watchtower in the background, and take turns standing on a narrow ledge that free-falls hundreds of feet to ocean-slapped rocks below.

·

Will is staying in Liscannor, and just as we are about to part ways at the crossroads, he points to a small roadside pub and offers to buy me a glass of Guinness.

A man at the bar sings a song I know well from my mother's records, "The Star of the County Down," and another accompanies him on a tin whistle. A small, very old man with loose pants suspended up to his chest begins to dance, slipping once on beer. Another man grabs him by the arm as he is falling and tries to guide him to a chair to sit down, but the old one refuses and continues his jig. As Will and I clap encouragement, he beams at us.

The dance ends and we cheer, and as the little old man disappears into a group on one side of the bar, a different man bursts into song in a high tenor, a slower, moodier air, the glasses on a nearby shelf shaking with the force of his vibrato.

> *Oh, Mary, this London's a wonderful sight*
> *With people all workin' by day and by night.*

Will and I stand so we can see the singer, a thickset man with a large forehead sitting on a barstool, a half-full pint glass in front of him.

> *Sure they don't sow potatoes or barley or wheat*
> *But there's gangs of 'em diggin' for gold in the*
> *street.*

I want to laugh, even as tears come to my eyes. The voice so earnest, so exposed in its pleading. There is something both controlled and unhinged about it.

> *At least when I asked them that's what I was told*
> *So I just took a hand at this diggin' for gold*

The singer's face is red, his eyes squeezed shut. The buttons strain at his shirt as he finishes the song:

But for all that I found there I might as well be
Where the Mountains of Mourne sweep down to
the sea.

•

It rains almost my entire walk back to Doolin. I'm soaked and a ways off from Tommo's when a tall man walking by with a dog comments to me: "It's a fine day for young ducks."

Surprised and delighted, I smile at him. It's an expression I can imagine my father using. The man then offers me his oilcloth coat to borrow until I get to my destination.

"I can't take your coat," I say.

"Ah, you're all right. Take it," he insists.

I thank him as he helps me on with it, then walks with me, just a step behind, his wiry gray dog loping ahead, then circling back to us.

When we pass the cottage where the goose lives, it honks at us from within a hutch where it is weathering the rain.

"That's Sally Devlin," the man says.

"The goose is named Sally Devlin?" I ask.

"Yes, and a right devil she is, too."

•

Standing under the awning at Tommo's in Doolin, soak-
ing wet, I watch the man in the oilcloth coat recede into
the distance, his dog dancing around him.

•

In my mother's drawer, a faded, slightly wrinkled prayer
card shows the Holy Mother in her most glorious aspect,
as she rises to heaven. Before a backdrop of overcast sky,
she stands on a cloud upheld by cherubs.

One of the Holy Mother's feet presses directly on the
head of a cherub, a fraught expression on his partially
faded face.

•

I've been getting anxious, unable to find someone to
hitchhike north with me to Yeats country.

At breakfast I approach Laura, a short, angular
Australian girl, after someone mentions to me that she
might be traveling north.

I've been watching her the past few days. Tommo's,
with its big communal tables, is not an easy place to
remain separate from others, yet she manages it. Her
dark hair always looks unwashed, and a patina of dust
surrounds her in her rugged frayed jeans and sweatshirt.
Her military green backpack is of an obsolete variety,
ripped and worn. She strikes me as a vagabond of sorts

and I am intrigued by the way she seems to guard her isolation. I suggest we travel together, surprised when she agrees.

She persuades me to take a detour first across the bay to the Aran Islands. The people there, Laura tells me, speak mostly Irish, and there are prehistoric stone forts on two of the islands that she wants to see. Since I've missed the chance to go with the Swiss girls, I agree.

•

The afternoon sky glows through a gauze of clouds as we cross Doolin Bay on a steamer, approaching Inisheer, the closest of the three Aran Islands, a sliver of barren limestone and white sand facing an uninterrupted expanse of the Atlantic to the west.

We secure a room at Flaherty's Bed and Breakfast and visit the old stone ruin of a castle on the single hill of the otherwise flat isle. From there, the strange austerity of the place is apparent, not a single tree anywhere, and hardly any people, a series of unmortared stone walls laid out in patterns to the south.

I felt a cold developing as we crossed the bay, and by evening, when Laura wants me to go with her to the pub, my throat is too sore and I have a headache. So she goes on her own while I lie in bed.

•

Under the summer shadows of trees on the backyard lawn, Dad throws the Frisbee with force and Rory, the half collie, bounds across the yard after it, leaps up at the perfect moment, and catches it in his mouth.

My siblings and I squeal and jump and stay on the sidelines, half in and half out of the sun, as Rory races back to Dad and drops the Frisbee at his feet. Dad scoops it up, holding it a moment aloft. Rory breathes hard, his back legs tense and trembling with readiness. Dad throws it and it soars.

•

Mom yells and Dad leaves the house. Rory goes to the screen door and watches Dad start the car. He waits there even after Dad has driven away.

•

Mom is upset and we don't want to stay home. The three of us girls are following Jerry, hiking through a big expanse of empty mesa. He's told us that the rodeo grounds are easy to sneak into before noon. He holds the barbed wire open wide and we each go through to the other side, where there are corrals and stables, bales of hay and fences with saddles on them.

"See," he says, "I told you! No one's here!"

A dusty brown-and-white Shetland pony with burrs in its heavy mane watches us from its stall.

We crowd the gate door, reach through, and pet the top and side of its head, the hair coarse and dry. It shakes its head up and down at us, and twitches its tall ears at buzzing flies.

•

I toss and turn under the blankets in Flaherty's Bed and Breakfast. To comfort myself I imagine that Denis is with me, our bodies entwined. Between kisses, he speaks Irish into my hair and neck.

•

Tracy and I are driving on a road that leads out of town on a cold February night when the battery in the Dodge Dart dies. A small red sports car pulls over and two handsome, long-haired guys get out to give us a jump. They're brothers from Illinois, on their way back from Mexico. After they get our car started again, we ask them if they want to smoke a joint. They say yes, and follow us as we drive along a desert road that leads to a stretch of mesa. We park, and when we turn the headlights off, it is dark, except for a sky filled with stars.

We pair up. Tracy and the taller one, whose name is Rick, sit together on the hood of the Dodge Dart talking, while I wander into the piñon trees with Justin. I have been fending off the loss of my virginity with the local boys, but Justin is from a faraway place, a place I can idealize because it is unknown, and because after this, he and his brother will keep driving north into the night. In spite of the cold, I take off my clothes and lay them on the ground, then lie down on top of them.

I can just make out his silhouette as he stands above me, taking off his pants. It is too dark to see his face as he lies over me, but I see it in my mind's eye, the way it looked in the headlights as he hooked the cables to our battery. I am smiling.

"I've never done this before," I say.

"Why not?" he asks.

"I just haven't."

"How old are you?" he asks.

"Sixteen. How old are you?"

"Twenty."

It hurts for only a moment and then the pain is gone. I touch his long hair that brushes my neck and the side of my face. I touch his arms and his strong back and stare up at the stars and pick out Orion's belt.

Driving home, I feel a shivery elation. I tell Tracy and she says she feels sick. Her repulsion confuses me. "You don't understand," I say. But she just wants to go home and get away from me. I try to explain but she won't listen.

In the bathroom, I examine the watery bloodstains on my inner thighs, then, gazing at my face in the mirror, tell myself that I've done something monumental.

I sneak out of the house and lie on the grass, dead now in winter, looking up again for the three stars of Orion's belt. I huddle in my coat, a deep cold coming up from the ground.

•

Laura is awake early and urging me to get ready to leave for the other two islands, but my sore throat is worse and I feel too weak and foggy-headed.

"Do you think you can come back for me tomorrow after you visit the other islands? We can take the ferry back across from here to the mainland, then go straight to Yeats country."

She looks into the air over my shoulder. I have become an inconvenience.

"I don't really want to come back to Inisheer once I leave."

"What if we meet tomorrow sometime on the big island, in the vicinity of the great stone fort?"

She agrees and says that late in the afternoon will be best. But I don't trust that she'll really try, and it worries me, so after breakfast, instead of going straight back to bed, I walk her to the wharf, trying to solidify details of meeting up. In spite of a sudden, furious rain, the steamer she gets on leaves. I weather the shower under a wooden awning, watching the boat disappear into fog. Ignoring the rain, two broad-shouldered young men stand on a boat that rocks alongside the pier, unwinding and preparing a mass of dark net. This seems an even more remote fisherman's life than one on the mainland coasts. The cold has me feeling vulnerable, both melancholy and euphoric. I can't seem to make myself stop watching them.

When the rain stops and their boat goes out, thin chickens emerge from little roosts in an empty wooden shack and peck on the wet sand.

•

I sleep for an hour, then wake agitated, though not sure why. As I lie there I feel almost certain that Laura won't meet me the next day. I am nervous about hitchhiking to Sligo alone and I wonder if I might be able to splurge on a bus. I take out my money and begin to count it. My heart sinks. I have not been keeping close tabs on my spending and I have much less than I thought. I saved a fifty-pound note separately from my other money for when I get back to Dublin, thinking it would tide me over until I had a job. But maybe I can use some of it for Yeats country.

I've been keeping the fifty-pound note in my journal. It's an older note of currency, a purple bill with Celtic knot-work detail, an image of Cathleen ni Houlihan in a shawl, peering over her shoulder at the viewer, the Lakes of Killarney in the background. I have been attempting to draw her. Opening the journal, I find my drawings, but the note itself is gone. In a panic, I take everything out of my backpack and search every possible place it could be three or four times, but to no avail. What I have left might cover me for another day of traveling, but without the fifty pounds I don't have enough for Yeats country. I'll have to go straight back to Dublin and try to find a job. It feels like a crime against my father, being so close to Yeats country and not being able to get there.

∙

I go with my father to the store and as he parks the car, I say, "Daddy, do you remember when we used to have parties in Yonkers and you would sing and recite poems?"

He smiles and furrows his brow. "You remember that?"

"Yes. Everyone wanted you to sing and recite. Everyone clapped for you."

He turns off the car, then nods, staring at the steering wheel.

"Why don't you do that anymore?"

"Oh, people do that kind of thing back East, not here. It's an Irish thing."

But then he is quiet. He gives me money and asks me to go in and get the things from the store.

∙

In spite of my sore throat and headache, I take a walk alone on the island through the narrow, turning pathways between the ancient unmortared walls, which protect small fields from the gales. Many of these little fields, I notice, have gone out of cultivation.

Because of the wind, the mist moves in big drifts like smoke, but it is so thick, I can see only a few feet ahead of me at a time. At a sudden turn, my heart jumps, as I find myself confronted by a figure seated on the wall, a red-haired boy, about eleven or twelve, with an elongated face, his eyes strange and pale behind red eyelashes. He wears a shirt and vest, and gray flannel pants much too large for him and rolled up, exposing his bare, dirty shins and callused feet.

I gasp, "You surprised me."

My own voice makes me self-conscious, and my words sound high-pitched and off-key, as I imagine he must perceive them. By the baffled stare on his face I am sure he speaks only Irish.

I move past him through the maze, turning back to see if he is still visible, but he is hidden in the mist.

On a storm beach level with the ocean, a massive weather-worn freighter leans to one side, beached on rocks, a few shreds of disintegrating rope still twisted on the masts. Except for big patches of rust, it is the same gray color as the sea and the stones it is beached on.

I walk as close to it as I dare, the low rocky shore at my feet, the inexhaustible sea roaring with tremendous force, beating at everything around it. I remain awhile, taking in the sweep of isolation and the wild, unexpected strangeness of all of it. As I stand in the wind, the boy's face haunts me.

•

On a Saturday morning, Jerry drives me to Tito's Market to get groceries. He waits in the car while I run in and when I come back and put the bags in the backseat, the air is filled with pot smoke. He doesn't talk to me much anymore. At home he stays in his room listening to records.

As he turns out of the parking lot onto Cerrillos Road, I ask him to stop at the Rock Shop, the place he was always pleading to go to when he was little. He seems reluctant and wants to know why.

"C'mon!" I say. "We haven't been there in such a long time."

It's colder inside than I remember it, with its cement floors and horned sheep skulls displayed on the walls. No one else is inside but a man in a cowboy hat sitting in a chair behind the cash register.

"Look, Jer," I say, and show him the fossil of a fish, its spine intricate, each rib clearly delineated. He looks at it with hazy, indifferent eyes.

•

Dad drives to Manny's Lounge, and parks. "I'll only be a minute," he says and goes in.

After fifteen minutes I am worried and tired of waiting. I get out of the car and go up to the entrance of the bar, gather my courage, grasp hold of the door, and pull. The air inside is shadowy and cool, almost chilly, and smells of maraschino cherries and whiskey. A multitude of bottles glimmer against a long mirror beneath a dark wood and red vinyl wall. I step inside and some of the men hunched over their stools turn and stare, the blurred shine of alcohol in their eyes. My father is among them but doesn't turn. I touch his shoulder. He looks up surprised and smiles at me.

"C'mon, Dad. You're taking too long."

An extra layer of light gleams on his eyes. "Crummy kid," he teases. "Why don't you have a Coke? Manny, give my daughter a Coke, and throw some cherries in it."

A man with a big red smirking face sits two barstools to the left of my father.

"Tony, this is my daughter Regina." He says my name slowly and musically.

"Hello, Regina," the man says, mimicking the way my father said it, like my name is a lyric in a song. His tiny, wet eyes rake my body. "Beautiful girl," he says.

"You hear that, Regina, you crummy kid?"

I turn and face my father, but I can feel the man's eyes on my back.

"Daddy, I don't want the Coke. Let's go," I urge.

"All right, all right," he says, still smiling, and stands, throwing cash on the bar.

Driving home, my father seems hardly there at all, coated in a glassy numbness.

"Don't tell your mother I stopped," he says as we pull into the driveway.

•

It is Mom's birthday and we give her a pair of pajamas and the album from the musical *Coco*. It must have been Dad who bought these things and Tracy and Sheila who wrapped them, because this is the first I know about them. After we give her the presents, she calls us all into the den and tells us to sit down. She brings a kitchen chair into the middle of the room, then drapes the new pajamas over the chair. Taking a bottle of iodine out of her pocket, she splashes it all over the pajamas. Tracy gets up to run out of the room and Mom screams at her to sit down, that she isn't finished. She then takes the record album out of its sleeve and smashes it over the back of the chair.

"Barbara, for the love of Almighty God!" Dad says.

She turns and looks up at him, then reaches for his face, her fingernails penetrating, tearing his cheeks. Blood runs down in four streams on each side.

I wonder if it is happening quickly or slowly. Is it happening so fast that he can't get away?

•

In second-grade religion class, I raise my hand. "I saw a sign that said God is dead."

"Don't even repeat that!" Sister Concetta cries and shakes her head. But I can tell that she's heard it before.

I realize it is not a secret, this idea that God is dead.

•

Dad is still not home. I think of the four deep cuts on each cheek, how he stood still, blood dripping down, staining his white shirt. He left the house without cleaning himself up.

The whole day passes and my father does not come back. I notice that he left his wallet on the side table. He has no money, wherever he is. But he has to come back for this. He has to come back. Out the window, the street is dark, except for the occasional headlights of passing cars, visible through the leaves of the poplars.

My father's wallet smells of tobacco, metal, and dull leather. The soft, worn wallet grows warm in my hands. I put it down on the coffee table and it seems to sleep there.

•

In the evening, I scale the hill to the pub, where I sit alone at a table near a window. Mrs. Flaherty has given me aspirin, and the pounding in my head is less. Now and then I remember the fifty pounds and wonder if Laura might have taken it. My pulses thrum with anger at the idea.

It is not yet dark out, but already the islanders who do not use electricity are lighting their kerosene lamps.

I wave to a Dublin couple, Finbar and Eileen, who are also staying at Flaherty's. They join me. They have been here three days, and Finbar, lanky and sandy-haired, talks about the ruggedness of the isles and the fact that there are no trees, only the maidenhair ferns that grow between the stones. Eileen, who has a heart-shaped face and curly dark hair, says that Connemara, the mainland shore east of the big island, is also treeless and barren, all rock. She quotes someone famous who said that the rough-hewn Aran Islands are "fragments of Connemara, flung offshore."

When I tell them that I am an actress and I'll soon be moving to Dublin, they describe the pubs in Temple Bar near the quays, where the theater people gather, and tell me about the Project Arts Centre, which does innovative Irish theater. I write these things down on a piece of paper and put it in my purse.

"You're flushed," Eileen says and puts her hand on my forehead the way my mother used to when she thought I might be feverish. When she orders me a hot toddy for my sore throat—Irish whiskey, boiling water, a spoonful of sugar, and four or five cloves—and promises it will also help my headache, I am convinced that she is one of the warmest people I've met in Ireland and tell her so. She smiles and when she puts her arm around me a moment, I rest my head on her shoulder.

•

It is morning when Dad comes back looking frazzled and exhausted. "I'm only here to get my things," he says. The cuts on his face have formed thick, dark scabs. He is shaking, and I think it must have to do with the fact that he is about to see my mother, and like all of us, from moment to moment, doesn't know what he will encounter.

"Don't go," I say to him and he meets my eyes.

He seems as lost as I am about what to do, as uncertain about what is ahead.

"Stay home, Daddy, please."

It seems to matter to him, my saying this. I put my arms around him and hold hard. His breath pauses. I sense, with a shock, his awareness of my breasts, of my body, and I am flooded with shame. Impending womanhood makes me desperately sad.

I break the hug and to hide what I am feeling, repeat the word, "Stay!"

We stand in silence. His eyes are heavy with exhaustion.

My mother comes calmly down the hall.

"You should get some sleep," she says.

My father sighs, the suspense over.

He sleeps in their bedroom with the door closed, while my mother sits in the living room drinking coffee.

Later in the afternoon, I look into my parents' room. There are four thin streaks of blood on the pillowcase where the scabs must have opened while he slept.

•

Eileen and Finbar speak Irish to some locals, a dark-haired woman named Macha, who looks to be in her midtwenties, a quiet man I take to be her husband, and two other men, both talkative, probably in their thirties. Eileen explains that I'm American, and they regard me with interest.

Macha invites us along to a cottage set on the rocks over a pounding sea. There is no electricity and the only illumination comes from the burning hearth fire and a few kerosene lamps. The room is austere, the floor stone and earth. I imagine it is the cottage where Denis and I live in Tír na nÓg.

•

We sit in a circle on rough cane chairs, the backs tied and formed of some kind of sinewy rope. A fresh salmon boils in a black pot hanging from a crane over the fire. I am the first to be given a piece when it is cut, and the first to be given a bottle of Guinness, which Macha's husband distributes.

"They're so gracious," I say to Eileen and Finbar. "But particularly to me."

"We're strangers, too," Finbar says, "but you're from a far shore and don't speak the language so you're the real guest."

"Only the crude and lowborn would be ungracious to a guest," Eileen adds.

"You never know with whom you break bread," Finbar says and winks. "For all they know, you could be a saint."

One of the talkative men sings a ballad in Irish while the other man holds his hand, turning his arm over and over in a circle as if he were winding him up. Everyone listens with absorption. Eileen translates for me in a whisper. The song is about fifteen Aran men who are fishing for black pollock from a high rock terrace in August 1852 on the Feast of the Blessed Virgin. A monstrous wave rises from the sea and swallows all of them, a consequence, some believe, for working on the holy day.

Macha's husband tells a story in Irish. In a whisper, Eileen explains, "He says he met an archangel on the road in Kilronan."

Macha tells us that earlier in the century, and not that many years since, when Aran people left to immigrate to America, wakes were held for them because in most cases they'd never return to Aran, and so never be seen again. But the emigrant ships that sailed out of Galway Bay for America had to wait sometimes for days in the lee in the southeast part of the big island for a favorable wind. And so the loved one might be seen again on the ship, but at a distance, visible but untouchable, waving to those being left behind.

"Like seeing a ghost," Eileen whispers.

•

I don't go home on my seventeenth birthday. I hear from different people at the college that my mother and father have been looking for me.

I'm sitting in a Pizza Hut, sharing a pizza with another girl, Hattie, whose dorm room I sometimes stay in, when my father appears.

"Come home, Regina. Let's go," he says.

"But look, Dad. We just got this pizza."

"I'll wait in the car while you finish," he says.

I ask the waiter if there is a back way and escape. I stand behind a building farther up Cerrillos Road and see my father go inside again. A few minutes later he storms out, gets in his car, and drives away.

Later when I am back in Hattie's dorm room, the phone rings.

"It's your father," she whispers.

"Hello," I say.

"Don't ever come home," he says. "I never want to see you again."

I go home an hour later and apologize to him. With little energy, he accepts.

•

"There's a mosquito somewhere in the car," Dad tells me.

As he turns onto Cerrillos Road, I notice the mosquito on my wrist, but before I can slap it, it's gone.

"It bit me," I cry.

Dad is giving me a ride to the college, and we drive the short distance in silence. I think of how I betrayed him only days before, made a fool of him. First Nanny treated him horribly, then Mom, and now me. I know he is still hurt, that he hasn't forgiven me. There is an awful resignation in him. I want to say something to fix what I've done.

He pulls over in front of the building where my first class is, then says, "Look!" He gestures with his head to his hand, which clutches the steering wheel. The mosquito is poised on his finger.

"Why are you letting it bite you?" I ask.

He doesn't react, but watches it. On impulse, I lean over and slap the mosquito, still on his finger. Dad winces. The mosquito is crushed, blood smeared on his knuckle and on the palm of my hand.

He stares at the blood. "Some of that is your blood," he says, waiting a few moments before reaching into his pocket and taking out his handkerchief, then wiping the blood and dead mosquito off his hand. He crumples the handkerchief with the smashed mosquito still inside it, and puts it back in his shirt pocket. "There's a poem by John Donne called 'The Flea,' about two people bitten by the same flea."

His mood lightens as he tries to remember the words. "We are met and cloistered in these living walls of jet . . ."

I tremble with hopefulness, the lines suggesting a closeness between the poet and the person being addressed. A poem might help heal the rift between us.

"One blood . . . made of two . . ."

About to continue, he takes in a breath, his mood still elevating.

"The flea is . . . our marriage . . ." He stops, not completing the line, as if he's run into a wall. He drops his eyes and seems not to breathe.

It isn't me in the poem with him anymore.

I reach for the handle of the door, but I don't open it. A cloud crosses the sun so we are left in shadow. It seems a long time we sit this way. When the cloud passes, the sun is so bright that the metal on one of the windshield wipers glints and briefly blinds me. I want to break the spell but don't feel able to. Finally he coughs and turns on the radio.

One blood made of two . . .

It requires great effort to reach into the backseat for my bag. He keeps his eyes fixed straight ahead through the windshield. I picture a tiny pinpoint of blood leaking through the pocket of his thin white shirt where the crumpled handkerchief is stuffed.

•

I go through the card catalog in the college library and find a volume of John Donne's poems that contains "The Flea," then look for an isolated place to sit and read. At the very back of the library, a vast window faces out across a long stretch of wild grass. I can see passing cars and hear the distant noise of engines.

I find the words that broke my father down:

> *This flea is you and I, and this*
> *Our marriage bed, and marriage temple is.*

I close my eyes and picture the tiny pinpoint of blood on my father's shirt pocket.

•

I leave the library and walk. I cannot stop thinking of the mosquito, a fragile and intricate creature, poised so purposefully on my father's finger. How easily, how negligently I crushed it.

•

Back at Flaherty's, my sore throat keeps me another night from sleep. Throughout the dark hours I hear a dog barking without urgency.

•

My father's four brothers, big, gently inscrutable figures, arrive from back East for the funeral.

I gather the facts I have about my father: He was the youngest of five boys. His father died when he was four, and his mother supported them by working as a cleaning woman during the Great Depression. John, the oldest, six years older than my father, virtually raised him.

I press them for more details. I learn that because my father's intelligence scores were so high, he worked during the Korean War breaking enemy codes. I want more, more personal memories of him, more details of his life, but all I get are vague abstractions, things I already know: *Your father was well-read. He was a very erudite man. He was charismatic.*

"Are there any memories you have? Any important things you can tell me about my father?"

"He was idealistic," one of them says. "He thought the world was his oyster."

•

On the bulletin board in my fifth-grade classroom, Sister Bernetta has tacked up a postcard she received from another nun who went to visit Notre Dame Cathedral in Paris.

On the card is an image of a reliquary, an elaborate, silver, coffin-like box containing the leg bone of Saint Vincent of Saragossa. The yellowing bone can be seen through a glass window, lying on a red velvet pillow.

•

When I leave Inisheer very early in the morning to visit the other two islands, turf fires burn along the shore. We lift sail in a good breeze just as the sun arrives, the gray overcast weather utterly gone. I can see in every direction.

The horizon to the west is endless, without a definite demarcation between sea and sky, and the mainland to the east, cliffs and lowlands, beach and rocks.

We soon dock at Inishmaan, which we tour on foot, a small group of us led by a tall, long-limbed Galway man named Michael Slattery, who asks us to call him Mick. We pass limestone cottages issuing smoke, fragrant of both earth and kelp. Curious children watch us from doorways. Indolent cows graze in fields congested with wildflowers.

Mick tells us that the three islands have four or five dark-haired families said to be descended from seals, and that less than a decade before, the local priest drove a witch from these shores.

After viewing gravestones defaced by weather, druid altars, and prehistoric forts overgrown with moss and lichen, we go on to the big island. Walking along roadways in the brightness, I search for signs of Laura, but she is nowhere to be seen. Mick remarks that the island is curiously empty of tourists for such a fine day.

I take out my map of Ireland and draw a tiny dot on the north point of the northernmost Aran Island. This is where I am in the world right now, ocean all around me. I look toward Galway Bay to the east, its circle of water washing into the Atlantic, where my grandfather and uncle Michael set sail for America.

•

It is my turn to pay my respects at my father's coffin. I am holding an envelope with poems inside, written on loose-leaf paper, five or six rambling pages. Much of it feels more like stammering than poetry. I have borrowed one line from "The Flea": *Our two bloods, yours and mine, mingled be.*

My father does not look like himself. I recognize part of his forehead and one of his temples, his hair, his ears, his hands. It infuriates me that the mortician, or whoever has put my father's face back together, has gotten it so wrong. The nose especially outrages me. It is pointed, not my father's Irish nose at all.

My mother whispers that I should put the envelope into his pocket. The fabric of his suit jacket sends a numb vibration through my fingertips as I lift it. My hand hesitates against his chest. I don't want to leave. I focus on my father's temple, which looks unaltered. "Can I kiss him?" I ask my mother. She nods. Even with a quick brush of my lips, I can feel the tremendous cold weight of his dead body.

•

This does not feel like a dream. I am waiting for my father at a scheduled meeting place that is neither inside nor outside. He has, somehow, arranged our meeting. A lot of people are around and a train arrives and my father gets off it, excited and clearly relieved to see me. We sit together at a long sort of cafeteria-style table. He is shak-ing, anxious, but seems hopeful that I can help him.

"Where do I go now?" he asks, leaning forward across the table, almost smiling.

"You are dead," I say.

"Yeah, I know," he says though he seems uncertain. "But I'm lost. I don't know where I'm supposed to go."

"I don't know, Dad," I reply.

He presses me, telling me that if I try, I will have the answer, but I don't. He panics. He gets up and heads for an elevator full of people. I run after him and just as the doors are closing, he says, "Reggie, I'm going to hell."

•

I discover that I can draw on the air with the Fourth of July sparkler that Dad lights and hands to me. The circle I draw on the air is green. Dad calls it *phosphorescence*. I write my name in script, but by the time I've written the last letter, the first one has faded to white and then dis-solved. Next I write *Dad*, and the entire word floats there a moment in green before going white and disappearing.

•

After the funeral I sit on my bed sewing, repairing a tear in one of my blouses. For a moment the air gets warmer, then collapses into a shock of cold that smells like snow or rain and something like rotting apples. I'm afraid to look up, so I stare at the needle poised between my thumb and forefinger. A fine, soft aura of white falls over my lap and hands, as if there is another light source in the room. I hear a soft, hoarse noise like something rustling, very dry cloth, tulle or net, dragging on wood. This is my father breathing.

I hang my head and start to cry, the tears so hot on my face they burn. He wants something from me. I feel him pulling at me. I say nothing, just weep. But he doesn't go.

•

I am nearing Dun Aengus, climbing to the promontory of the ancient monument, magnificent and barbaric, three concentric massive stone walls built on a precipice and curved to form and protect a great system of a fortress.

"We know from bardic writings that centuries before the birth of Christ, a civilization similar to Homer's thrived here and remained up until the coming of Saint Patrick," Mick says, then goes on to explain that the fortress's placement on the high ground of the island allows for an ultimate view all around.

Ditches, palisades, and borders of sharp, upturned rocks jut in all directions, like a wall of jagged stone soldiers that made passage impossible to Viking marauders.

We wander through a crude, narrow stone doorway into what was once a city. Some walls are in ruins, while others stand mighty, many of them fifteen or twenty feet thick. On the easterly side, the circular wall stops at the edge of a cliff that descends hundreds of feet to the ocean.

Mick advises us to lie on our stomachs, to look straight down. Even doing this, I am overcome with vertigo, and have to close my eyes and belly-creep backward.

As we begin our descent, he points out other small forts and raths along the way that he says are older still than Dun Aengus, built by the mysterious people known as the Tuatha de Danaan, "tribes of the goddess Danu," who conquered Ireland with magic. But the druids were too powerful for them and the Tuatha de Danaan fled and took refuge in these raths and forts, which are now called fairy mounds.

"There are people these days who romanticize the pagan druids," Mick adds. "But they weren't harmless tree worshipers, as is popularly believed. They performed human sacrifices."

Just as he begins to lead us away, he turns and points westerly and slightly north into the Atlantic. "That, it is said, is where Tír na nÓg lies."

•

I persuade my mother and sisters to go with me to the movies to see the new version of *The Great Gatsby*, with Mia Farrow and Robert Redford. Neither my sisters nor I have read the book. Our mother has, but long ago, and she has forgotten that there is a suicide at the end, or maybe she just doesn't expect it to be so graphically depicted in the film, the man putting the gun into his mouth. After we get home, Tracy retreats to her room, and Mom and Sheila sit together on the couch, neither speaking, but clinging to each other. I apologize for having suggested the movie. "You love Robert Redford," I say to my mother. "I just wanted all of us to go to a movie."

Sheila joins Mom in her room that night to watch old movies on television and even sleep there. The two of them curl up against each other, not like mother and child, but like two children.

•

In our living room on Park Hill, my father, young, dark-haired, and smiling, recites poems and everyone listens. The second he stops, thunder sounds. People cheer. A moment later, there's a downpour.

"Vincent!" a man cries. "You brought the rain!"

"God love you," says a sweating woman who is fanning herself with a magazine.

"God love you, Vincent," another woman echoes.

•

I am staring at the horizon when Mick calls out to me from a distance. They all stand there in a little group, waiting on me. I follow them to the shore, where we get onto a steamer, which speeds, skipping the water, toward Galway Bay. I stand in the full blast of the wind and sun, still looking to the west.

I tell myself that after getting to Galway, I will take a bus back to Dublin. But I stop awhile on the pier, looking for the rocks my grandfather and uncle Michael had been standing on when the photograph was taken. So much time has passed. Those rocks have probably long since shifted or fallen into the water. And I realize now that the old photograph was so insubstantial, the picture itself a ghost, two pale, sepia figures partially erased in a blitz of white light.

•

I buy my ticket and there is an hour yet before I can board so I walk through a maze of nearby streets.

Galway is different from any other Irish town I've been to. There is a Spanish influence to the architecture, many of the bookshops and cafés colorfully painted, with lanterns and courtyards and arched doorways, and some of the shops with the word *Spain* or *Spanish* in the name.

In a bookstore window there is a portrait of Yeats. It pains me again that I cannot get to Yeats country, as if I have broken a promise to my father.

As I pass the open door of a pub, a tin whistle plays a mournful melody, and I stop to listen. When the last note ends, a flood of fast-paced, merry music, fiddle and bodhran and flute, takes over the air. A man sings in a high-pitched, nasal voice:

> *In the first of me downfall I put out the door,*
> *And I straight made me way on for Carrick-on-*
> *Suir.*
> *Radley fall da diddle ai,*
> *Radley fall da diddle ai-o.*

•

"Do you think . . . is it my fault . . . what happened to your father?"

My heart throbs in my throat. I can't get rid of the image of my mother scratching my father's face with every ounce of energy in her body, tearing four deep cuts into each cheek. I shake all over. I want to say, *Yes. It's your fault.*

With great effort, I say, "No."

•

I go to Eyre Square and sit on a bench in view of the public clock to keep track of the time so I won't miss the bus, but soon find out that it is delayed another hour. In a little restaurant called the Port of Spain, I sit at a table near an open French door. A waitress, around my age, with black, spiky hair, wearing a T-shirt with the phases of the moon on it, takes my order: a glass of Harp Lager and a package of peanuts. I chug most of the beer in one long swig, then ask her if my backpack will be safe where I've left it if I go to the bathroom. She says she'll keep an eye on it.

As I am coming back, I stop to study a dartboard with a familiar historical face on it, one dart stuck into a mole on the right side of the man's mouth, hundreds of tiny dart punctures all over his face.

I realize who it is.

"Can I throw a dart at him?" I ask the waitress, who is standing near the bar. "Do I have to pay for it?"

"Have a throw," she says. "On the house."

Remembering Denis's instructions, I focus the dart. "A pox on you, Oliver Cromwell," I cry as I throw it and it sticks hard in his chin.

"Damn it," I say. "I was going for his eye."

She laughs. "He's made mincemeat of so often, we have to get replacements every few weeks."

"Good," I say.

I go back to my table to finish my lager and peanuts and the waitress comes with a full pint glass of Harp. "This is on the house," she says. "For knowing your Irish history. You'd be surprised how many Yanks come over here and have no idea who Oliver Cromwell was."

"Thank you so much," I say.

"Not at all," she says. "No manager on duty tonight. While the cat's away . . ." She winks at me.

•

On the bus to Dublin I find the fifty-pound note folded up and zipped into a side pocket in my jacket and have a vague memory of putting it there while I was still in Doolin. But what kind of a fugue state have I been in that I couldn't remember this? I decide that I will get off the bus. I can easily go back to Galway, then find my way to Sligo. But when the bus stops, I am overcome with inertia, leaning hard against the window and staring out. My body refuses to budge.

I half close my eyes. I want to sleep, to temporarily disappear. I cannot fathom this act of sabotage I am committing against myself.

I am destined, over and over, to keep losing my father.

•

Dad's driving, I'm riding shotgun, and Jerry's in the backseat, when "Whole Lotta Love" by Led Zeppelin comes on the car radio.

"Yay!" I say.

"Turn it louder, Reg!" Jerry says.

I reach over and turn up the volume. When Robert Plant screeches a loud, undulating "Lo-o-o-o-o-o-ve!" over guitar distortions, Dad says, "Christ!" and turns it down.

"Dad!" I exclaim.

"That's the tune the old cow died of," he mutters.

I pretend I'm still mad, but have to turn my face away from him so he won't see that I'm holding back a laugh.

•

Mom lights cigarettes, smokes them for a little while, then leaves them on counters or shelves. I find them on the window ledges, sometimes dangerously close to a curtain, funnels of ash that leave deep burns on the wood or the tile.

In the living room she faces the piano and stares. Everything I say to her has to be repeated five, six, seven times. It is like shouting down a tunnel. It takes time and energy to reach her and even then when she turns to me, she can't concentrate enough to answer.

I focus on titles on the bookshelf: *The Ox-Bow Incident, Ivanhoe, The Mystery of Edwin Drood*.

We sit in silence, she in her brown chair facing the wall above the piano, me on the couch, hunched forward in an uneasy suspense.

Jude the Obscure. Little Dorrit.

She turns in my direction and says, "My father . . . they say his death was a car accident, but I think he drove deliberately off the road."

I know he died when she was fifteen. I know he drank.

My eyes stop on a thick, worn textbook from high school English, a collection of Greek dramas. I remember a title: *The Fall of the House of Atreus*.

I get up and go out into the front yard to breathe. The poplars encircling our house move back and forth in the wind. They shudder in unison like a Greek chorus.

•

In one of Blake's etchings, God sits with a man on a cloud and points down at a horrific monster standing on the earth below. "Behold now Behemoth," God says, "which I made with thee."

•

My father is dead and my mother is in the hospital. My sisters and I keep the house lit at night, the windows and doors open. We turn the stereo on loud. Over and over again we play "Baba O'Riley" by the Who, singing the repeated chorus about teenage wasteland, and each time Roger Daltrey does the wild, uninhibited, drawn-out scream, we all do it with him, as if to invite one of the neighbors to come see what's going on. We want to upset someone. We want them to complain.

But no one comes.

None of us can sleep. The trees in the yard are in their late summer fullness, tumultuous and rushing, the lawn neglected, green and long as meadow grass. We get in the car barefoot at 1:00 AM to go for a ride.

Few cars are on the road at this hour. In the dark, we drive up Galisteo, an old, narrow Santa Fe street lined with ancient cottonwood trees, the radio blasting "Stairway to Heaven." We sing it with elation, the wind through the open car windows blowing our hair.

We decide on an impulse to sneak into the hospital. It is full of shadows and silence, broken by stations of light. We walk through, passing each checkpoint undetected. A guard disappears into a back room or an administrator's head turns as a phone rings. We reach the elevator and go to the third floor, where a trio of matronly nurses stand, conferring with one another like the Three Fates. They speak in half voices right in front of us, yet we pass them unseen as if something mystical propels us forward. Mom's door is ajar, her dark room lit only by the fluorescence from the hallway. We surround her bed.

"Mom," I whisper and she opens her eyes, startled out of a drugged sleep.

"We love you, Mom, we love you," Tracy and Sheila chime in.

The three of us repeat the chant again and again, hugging her, looking into her face. "We love you. We love you."

"I love you," comes her slow voice, a register deeper than usual. She looks as if she thinks she might be dreaming this.

In the doorway, the Third Fate, Atropos, she who cuts the thread of life, appears. "What are you doing here at this hour? You've got to leave."

"She's our mother," I say.

An anguished expression comes over the big woman's face as she insists again that we leave. "We love you, Mom. We love you." She nods, at a loss. We are ushered out. The clock says twenty-five minutes after one. We drive home without any giddy moments. We are tired. There are tears.

PART FIVE

D id you see County Clare?" the woman in the shop on Dawson Street asks. "Did you see the Cliffs of Moher?" She comes out from behind the counter and stands before me, a short energetic creature with a wide, freckled forehead. The morning before I left for the West, I stopped here to buy ten Silk Cut cigarettes and a Cadbury bar.

"Yes! So beautiful!"

"Ahhhh!" she says and laces her fingers together, her eyes a riot of light behind her glasses. "I miss it!"

I tell her all the places I went and show her postcards I have in my purse.

Before I leave she takes a chocolate-covered biscuit filled with jam from a cake dish on the counter, wraps it in a small piece of wax paper, and hands it to me.

"Take it, love! Take it!"

•

Willing to overlook her disapproval of my backpack, Theresa lets me stay at Fatima House at a reduced rate. While I do not get the full Irish breakfast that the regular guests get, she gives me tea and toast every morning in the drafty breakfast room.

•

I have just left the pool in the brand-new complex on Cerrillos Road where I am sharing an apartment with Wendy, who is back from Connecticut for the fall semester. It feels good to be away again from my childhood house. As I near my front door, I spot the white Rambler station wagon approaching on the shimmering tarmac. The car turns and pulls into a parking spot, the chrome around the windshield flashing in the hot sun, hurting my eyes so I have to shield them. Mom, Tracy, and Sheila have come to visit, to see the apartment for the first time. They follow me, almost mechanically, into the front room that still smells of paint and cheap construction.

I close the door. In the cool, dim interior, the heaviness of their collective mood infiltrates everything. For a moment, we all stand and stare into the mostly empty, carpeted space around us.

I speak with forceful cheer, offering ice water, but only Tracy accepts. She is wearing one of my cast-off shirts, her thick, wavy hair tied back in a ponytail. She sits cross-legged on the carpet, a baffled openness in her expression as she reaches up and receives the cup.

Sheila sits on Mom's lap in Wendy's new rocking chair, arms wrapped around Mom's neck, bare legs hanging over the side as her cheek adheres to Mom's chest. One of her yellow flip-flops falls off her foot and lies overturned on the floor.

I chatter about the pool. It's usually crowded with noisy little kids, but if we go at the right hour, it's almost empty. "You should bring your suits one day soon and we'll all swim."

None of them has anything to share, so I tell them how, at my waitress job in the coffee shop at the King's Rest Motel, I waited on our old pediatrician, Dr. Harris.

When Mom says nothing, I add, "He ordered a steak."

Mom points to a pack of tarot cards, which are sitting on the side table. They are Wendy's, I explain. "She's taught me how to use them. It's fun."

There is a silence.

"Will you do a reading for me?" Mom's voice drags like a record being played at too slow a speed.

I hesitate but she asks again, and then I think that maybe this could be positive, that I could tell her that good things are going to happen.

I hand her the deck and tell her to shuffle it. When she gives it back I ask her to pick one card from anywhere within and it will be the significator for her reading.

She pulls one out and turns it over: the Hanged Man. Her mouth falls slack and she raises her eyes to meet mine.

"This card does not mean the obvious. This is a positive card."

My blood rises as I watch Mom sink further. Sheila's expression, the side of her face pressed to Mom's chest, matches the subtle change.

"This card is about renewal," I insist.

She doesn't believe me.

I tell her to shuffle. I lay the cards in a pattern and read them according to Wendy's instructions.

I tell her the reading is positive and that it suggests that a difficult time is coming to an end, but a sad resolve has formed on her brow. She stares at the Hanged Man at the center of the spread.

Sheila closes her eyes and her jaw goes limp as if she is sleeping. Tracy runs her fingers back and forth in the shag of the carpet.

"It's positive," I tell Mom, trying to hide my anger. "It's saying that everything will be okay if you try. But you have to try. Do you know what I mean?"

Her focus is not on me, but past my shoulder, her pupils suddenly tiny as if something incredibly bright has appeared there. I feel dizzy. Is she seeing Dad?

"Mom," I call out. "Mom."

When she finally looks at me again, she narrows her eyes as if she is trying to remember who I am.

•

Coming in to Fatima House one afternoon I notice that there is a light on in the big room where breakfasts are served. I hear soft female voices and walk quietly over. Theresa and her nine-year-old daughter are at one of the tables drawing pictures together. Theresa looks as absorbed as her daughter, coloring something diligently with an orange crayon.

"Mam, can I have the greenish-blue one, the one like turquoise?"

"Yes, love." Theresa picks the crayon from a pile and hands it to her.

•

It is Theresa who, having come to my room to tell me her woes, suggests I apply at the Harp on O'Connell Bridge, a popular complex of pubs that also serves sandwiches.

I am hired to work six shifts a week for thirty-five pounds cash paid every Saturday. I begin right away. I'm not trained or told where anything is, just put behind the bar and expected to serve. Some Dublin accents are so strong I have to ask people to repeat their orders more than once, and it doesn't help that people are asking for things I've never heard of. I have no idea what a *Britvic orange* is, or a *Babycham*, or that *white lemonade*, often requested, is basically Sprite. If no fellow worker is nearby to ask, some of the customers seem to know where everything is kept behind the bar and direct me themselves. Most seem not to mind, but some are vaguely irritated. I hear one man tell another, "She's fit to mind mice at a crossroads." And though I've never heard the expression before, I know it cannot be a compliment.

·

The postal strike, which has been plaguing Ireland for eighteen weeks, is now over. I gather together the postcards I've written for my siblings and consider dropping them all into the box on Gardiner Street. But the Dublin mailboxes have been unused for so long because of the strike that I'm afraid to trust them. I have been warned that the mail will be a mess, most likely, for a while yet.

I take the postcards directly to the general post office on O'Connell Street. The place is pandemonium, a confusion of shouts and echoes, mountains of letters and papers in vats being rolled across polished tile floors in every direction. Still, in spite of my trepidation, I put all my cards into the proper slot. I leave, hoping I did the right thing, wondering if they'll all be lost.

I dream that night that I've made a terrible mistake. I've traveled so far away that there is no possibility of getting back. The nightmare makes me sit up in bed, and it takes twenty minutes or more with the light on for the panic to wane.

•

In a bookstore, I find large volumes with beautiful photographs of Yeats country and of County Kerry. There are several taken in Ballyferriter, on Clogherhead Beach with views of Sybil Head and the Three Sisters.

In one photograph I see a tiny fleck midway up the rise of a hill, and I'm sure it's the cottage. An itinerant woman lived there for a year or two, Denis said. It would not be impossible.

•

I work three consecutive nine-hour days at the Harp and arrive back at Theresa's around eight on a Saturday night, exhausted and miserable, looking forward to sleeping in on Sunday.

She greets me at the door and tells me that I have just missed a telephone call from Denis O'Connor.

"Did he leave a number?" I cry.

"No."

"What did he say?"

"He just asked for you and I told him you were working."

I imagine him somewhere in Dublin with his friends, in a pub where I could be dancing with him or embracing him at that miserable moment. I could be with him.

I almost want to run outside and look for him, but that is crazy. Where would I go? He never mentioned a particular street or pub in Dublin. I'll miss him if he calls back. It's unbearable.

Pacing back and forth, I start to cry.

Disapproving of my urgency and emotion, Theresa begins to lecture me that this is not the way to behave with a man, that I should not wait near the phone, that men don't like a girl who is too anxious. I cry, though I struggle not to. I tell her I understand but that I am going to wait near the phone. She says all right, but she won't allow me to leave the light on, that her bills are too high.

"You can't treat the electricity as if it's a birthright." She brings me a candle and lights it. "Don't carry it around," she says. "Don't bring it anywhere near the curtain."

I pace back and forth in the candlelight, hugging myself, staring at the silent phone and pleading with it to ring.

After midnight I blow out the flame and, aided by the glow of a street lamp through the window high above the front door, make my way through the dark to the big Georgian staircase. I fall into a troubled sleep in which I dream dozens of small spiders come out of the lines in my palms and run up my wrists and all over my arms.

I am off on Sunday and while I sit in the breakfast room having tea, I say to Theresa, "I wish he had said where in Dublin he was staying."

"He's not in Dublin," she says. "The call was long-distance."

I gape at her. If I had known this I'd have spent an easier night.

•

I ask Theresa if I can call him at the number in Ballyferriter he'd written in my address book, and pay her whatever the call costs. She says yes, and pretends to go, but I can see her shadow on the floor outside the door, which she has left ajar. I don't think Denis will answer and it stuns me when he does.

"Did you see Yeats country?" he asks.

"I didn't get to it," I say. "I misplaced fifty pounds." I tell him I had to come back and get a job and that now I am working at the Harp on O'Connell Bridge.

"Will you be coming soon?" I ask.

"No, I can't come straightaway. That's why I called." He says that the *Johnny Ruth* is on its way up to Killybegs and he's signed on to go with them.

I struggle to hold back my disappointment. I ask when he thinks he might be able to come. "I don't know," he says, pauses a few minutes, then adds, "but I'm going to try."

When I don't respond, he says, "It's nice to hear your voice."

I want to say all kinds of things, to tell him I miss him, to tell him that I hate Dublin and that I want to come to him, but I manage to hold back my hysteria.

He says that now that the postal strike is over he will write to me and that I should write him. I worry that he's winding up the conversation.

"There are some beautiful pictures of Ballyferriter in a bookstore here," I say. "I think there's a picture of that cottage, you know the one way up on the hill?"

"Is there?" he asks.

"I go by there and look at those pictures, and at pictures of Valentia Island, places where you and I walked together."

"It was a wonderful time that we had that night," he says.

"Yes, it was."

He says again that it's good to hear my voice and I reciprocate.

After we say good-bye, I go back upstairs, close the curtains, lie on my side, and weep. He seems to feel none of the urgency I do. I wonder if he is not telling me everything, that maybe it has something to do with what I told him about my parents, that it is too awful for him to accept. I wish I'd never told him.

I think about the itinerant woman who lived alone in that cottage and imagine myself living there, clearing out the shrubs and the overgrowth and chasing away the birds. I imagine lighting a fire at night and watching for Denis, waiting for him to arrive. I wonder what people said about that woman, if they thought she was a lunatic.

•

Searching through the *Irish Times*, I find a bedsitter flat in Glasnevin, on the north side on a dead-end street called Marguerite Road, for thirteen pounds a week, not a good rate I am told by others, but not obscene, either.

The building is redbrick, not a big Georgian like Theresa's, but on a smaller scale, one of a row of connected, nearly identical two-story houses. The foyer and hallway are pervaded by a gamey, fatty odor that hangs in the air and takes up residence in the wallpaper, an odor I will eventually identify as broiled mutton chops, cooked on an almost daily basis by a stout single woman in the flat closest to mine.

My flat, in the back on the first floor, is a bit worn, but clean. I have to use a communal bathroom in the hallway, and put a five-pence piece into a slot to heat up the water half an hour before I want a shower, but I have my own kitchen in a separate room, which I find out is a big plus. All the other flats in the house are single rooms with hot plates.

The walls of my main room are papered in gaudy orange and yellow. If it weren't faded, it would exhaust my eyes even being in the room. A small plug-in heater sits in a tiled half alcove beneath the mantel of a faux fireplace. There is beige carpeting and a big window with stiff curtains on a string pulley.

The very narrow bed has a white plastic cushioned headboard with a small tear in it, and the mattress, I will discover right away, is home to a peculiar kind of bedbug: tiny, pale, and fragile-looking with tall legs. They do not run away or hide when I expose them, but stand there in stupid defiance. A powder is sold that can be dusted beneath the sheet. It works, but stinks, irritating my sleep, so I sometimes wonder if it isn't better just to let the funny little bugs bite me.

•

"Tracy, wake up!" I whisper across the space between our beds.

I am ten and she is eight.

It's the middle of the night and I've had a bad dream. I have to go to the bathroom but I'm afraid to go alone.

She sits up without protest and gets out of bed, then walks shoulder to shoulder with me in the dark hall, holding my hand. In the bathroom I switch on the light, and covering her eyes with her hands, she sits on the edge of the tub and waits for me.

•

I write to Denis and give him my address and the phone number of the wall phone in the hall on the second floor.

I familiarize myself with the Finglas bus, which takes me to and from O'Connell Bridge, and struggle to make the best of my job at the Harp, even though it pays poorly and the fifty pounds I came back to Dublin with has quickly gone. After paying my rent and buying a few necessary things like a sheet and a towel, a pot, a pan, and a kettle, I have hardly enough to scrape by. I am trying to save money. I tell myself I will go back across Ireland and see Yeats country. But in the end I spend whatever I save on a chicken curry from the chip shop, or cigarettes, or a glass of lager with lime.

•

Theresa forwards a package of letters that all came to Fatima House for me, most from my siblings, full of news from their everyday lives. I try to read them in chronological order.

Tracy has sent two photographs, one of herself on the back patio in the apartment where she is now living. She's wearing shorts and a UNM T-shirt, looking sideways and squinting in the dusk light.

The picture of Sheila is not posed. She is caught midstride on the sidewalk, smiling and long-legged in her jeans.

In one of Tracy's letters, she tells me that Jerry is going to marry Karen, a friend of hers whom he had started seeing before I left New Mexico. They are all excited. Karen's parents are going to pay for the reception, which will be in Santa Fe at the Gates of Spain, a beautiful restaurant in the La Fonda Hotel.

The one letter I have from Jerry is from before he proposed. He mentions Karen, but mostly writes about his new job as a lineman.

I write to him and Karen right away, congratulating them, feeling anxious and guilty for not being there.

•

Dad and Jerry have put up a tent in the backyard so the three of us girls can have a campout. We put down air mattresses and cover them with blankets and pillows. Sheila brings in her stuffed animals. When she falls asleep, Tracy and I lie listening to my transistor radio and whispering.

The night is breezy, the grass tall and cool. There's a wild chorus of cricket song. We have left the flap open on the tent so we can see through the zipped screen.

The porch light switches on and Mom appears, a frenzied halo of moths around her. She comes across the grass to check on us.

•

Tracy tells me in a letter that when Jerry cleared out the house, he saved the old photo albums and now she is in possession of them, although no one knows what has become of any of the negatives. I write to her and ask her to send me pictures of our parents, old ones from when they were happy. There are two in particular that I ask her to try to find from just before they married. They had each taken a picture of the other in what looks like a garden outside a church.

I dream that my parents are laughing and speaking to me from the two photographs. I have the same buoyant feeling in the dream as I had on the ferry coming to Ireland, that they are proud of me for having come here.

A few weeks pass and I get a letter from Tracy asking if I received a large envelope she sent with old photos of Mom and Dad and a variety of other family photos. I worry that it may have been lost. Every day I come back to the flat, anxious to see if the envelope has arrived, and my heart sinks each time I find that it hasn't.

•

In makeshift tutus, Tracy, Sheila, and I are dancing in the living room to *Swan Lake*. Every time the pas de deux ends, I run over, lift the needle, and put it back on.

There is a rumble in the afternoon sky. Jerry rushes in and calls us outside to show us a massive cloud that is both dark and lit at once, like a lamp wrapped in a gray wool scarf.

"That's a thunderhead," he says.

We all exchange a wide-eyed look.

"A thunderhead," Sheila repeats.

We sit cross-legged on the unmown lawn and wait for a flash of lightning.

•

Weeks go by while I wait for the pictures. I spend much of my time reading novels and sitting in a corner on the bookstore floor looking at images of the West. I'm feeling more comfortable with my fellow workers at the Harp. I am a novelty because I am an American. Some of them talk wistfully about one day moving to America, and all of them, even those who do not want to leave Ireland, are fascinated by the United States, and they are all smitten with Hollywood. Westerns especially are very popular here, and they all get excited when I speak to them with a Texan accent.

"Howdy pawdner," I say. "I'll shoot at your feet until you dance." I have them all calling their shoes "shitkickers" and crying out, "Eeeeee-haaaahhh."

•

Our stick horses whinny and rear up on their hind legs before setting off again at a gallop. All four of us kids are riding back and forth the length of the backyard, our hearts beating faster and harder with each turn.

•

I cross a bridge over the Liffey. I wander, looking into shop windows, now and again going in. Inside a dark secondhand shop, a double brass picture frame faces the window, its two glass ovals refracting daylight. All the other frames lined up around it display photographs, mostly old sepias and watery black-and-whites, formal portraits of ordinary-looking people. But only dry dark blue velvet backing shows through the glass ovals of the double frame. How perfect it would be for the photos when they arrive.

"It came from a house near Dún Laoghaire Harbor," the proprietor, a soft old figure of an Irishwoman, says to me from another dim aisle where she is dusting porcelain. She explains that the winds over the Irish Sea likely caused the brass to go green with oxidation.

That adds to its appeal for me. It has been inundated with molecules of sea air.

"Oh," I say, picturing the double frame facing out a second-floor open window, two black-and-white pictures of my parents within it, their smiling faces gazing out at incoming tides. I reach for it. It is surprisingly heavy, its cool surfaces heating in response to my fingers. Its weight impresses me. It could be a kind of home for the pictures, hold them in place. But when I see the price on the back, I return it to its spot on the shelf and stroll slowly away from it. The only customer in the shop, I pause before archaic objects on display: a bellows for a fire, a fire screen carved with Celtic knot-work, a serving platter painted with leaping stags. But I only half look at these things. I am seeing my parents' faces in the double frame, the perpetually moving ocean reflecting on the glass.

"You're an American," the proprietor observes, though I haven't spoken more than a single word to her.

"Yes," I say and smile. Few Irish girls I've seen in Dublin, or even in the West, wear their hair long and untended as I do.

I gravitate back to the double frame, drawn to its solidity, two safe windows hinged permanently together, through which each could look, and through which each could be regarded.

"That was in the same house well over a century."

I jump slightly. The proprietor stands about a foot behind me, her slow brogue a persuasive music in the enclosed silence of the room. "But no one owns it now."

Her proximity unsettles me. I do not have the money to buy it.

I look at her guiltily, the lenses of her glasses, like the double frame, reflecting the light through the window.

I feel her disappointment as I thank her and leave.

Outside it occurs to me that it probably wasn't my long, straight hair that gave me away as an American. I've seen plenty of Scandinavian and German girls at the youth hostels and elsewhere who wear their hair long and loose.

I've been told that Americans come to Ireland looking for touchstones to the past, mooning after connections to a lost ancestral home. I moved through her shop of antiquated things as if I were in church.

•

It's dark out as the four of us board the Ferris wheel, our last ride of the day at the New Mexico State Fair. The car we're in ascends as kids board other cars. We stop for a long time when we're at the top of the wheel. Jerry rocks us back and forth. Everything looks beautiful from up here, all the colored lights of the fairgrounds below, and above and around us, the stars. Through the metal screen enclosure, I can see Mom and Dad far down on the ground below, two shadows looking up at us.

•

I venture one day to the theater department at Trinity College for advice about how to audition for plays in Dublin, and speak to a professor who encourages me to join the weekly Sunday acting group at the Focus, a highly regarded company that does Chekhov and Ibsen in a tiny, decrepit theater in Pembroke Alley near Leeson Street. It is led by a famous Dubliner, Deirdre O'Connell, an eccentric figure in long black dresses and shawls, her voluminous red hair always pinned up in the style of a Gibson girl. She studied at the Actors Studio in New York and fosters a Stanislavsky approach, similar to what Kim Stanley taught.

I am among a group of fifteen that meets weekly, a training period for possible company work. We do a variety of movement and improvisational exercises in a convivial atmosphere, both playful and serious. It is like sustenance to me, and I revel in every moment of the four hours I spend there each Sunday. I become friends with the other actors, three in particular. My Dublin life begins to fall into place.

•

Near the end of August, the IRA assassinates British admiral Lord Mountbatten in Sligo, and a few days later, while visiting dignitaries are on O'Connell Street, there is a bomb threat.

I am enlisted to stand at the door of the Harp and check ladies' purses for guns and bombs. I look at the manager who has given me the order, a plump, thirty-something man named Paddy, and ask, "Me?"

"Yes," he says and won't explain why I have been picked. So I have to do it, stand there and ask ladies to open their purses so I can look inside them. Men aren't searched. It's ridiculous. Someone says that I've been picked to do it because I'm a Yank, that people might be intimidated by an American accent. Between that and the long hours and low wages, I decide I have to find something better.

It is through someone at the Focus Theatre that I hear about a waitress job at Dobbins Wine Bistro, a Bohemian kind of place, where the hours are shorter and the money much better than anything I could make at the Harp.

I go for an interview and get the job.

It is a continental yet laid-back atmosphere, with flagstone floors and rustic exposed brick walls, a menu that offers seafood and steaks, and an extensive wine list.

After two four-hour dinner shifts, I make in wages and tips almost what I made in six nine-hour days at the Harp. I'll be able to put away a few pounds here and there for Yeats country.

I become close with another waitress at Dobbins, Letty Le Jeune, a sculptor, four years older than I am. Tall and dark-haired, she has the same propensity for silliness. On a slow night, we place a lit cigarette into the mouth of a whole salmon lying on a bed of greens on the salad bar. We watch the customers perusing the display to see their reactions. Most look askance at the salmon, smoke issuing from the cigarette. Some blink and stare a few moments, then dismiss it. After each reaction, Letty and I look away, stifling our laughter.

A tipsy woman weaves her way to the salad bar and lets out a surprised yelp, turns to us, and says, "Do you think if I asked him, he'd let me borrow that?"

I extract the cigarette from the fish's mouth and present it to her. Smiling, she hesitates a moment, then grabs it, takes a puff, and hands it back to me.

Letty and I sometimes go out to the pub after work, laugh a lot, then get into intense conversations about our artistic dreams, her about sculpture and me, acting.

•

After *Trojan Women* closes and I am making waitressing money again, I go to Doodlet's, a novelty shop downtown, and buy presents for Tracy and Sheila: a Russian wool scarf, green with bright red roses, for Sheila; a necklace for Tracy, small painted tin watermelon halves linked together. I drive to Albuquerque to see them.

Jerry is visiting them when I arrive.

Because I don't have a television, I am not familiar with *Monty Python's Flying Circus*, which the three of them keep referring to, red-faced and laughing. "There's a penguin on the telly!" Tracy cries in a high-pitched Cockney accent.

"Nudge, nudge, wink, wink!" Sheila responds.

"A nod's as good as a wink to a blind man!" Tracy counters back.

Jerry bellows in a deep voice, "I beg your pahhhhh-don!"

•

After working a lunch shift, I walk toward Temple Bar, and cross the Liffey at O'Donovan Rossa Bridge. Someone has told me about a tourist shop there where I might find out about tours to Yeats country. The travel agent is busy with a demanding customer but gives me a pamphlet with all sorts of information about various tours and accommodations in Yeats country. When I leave, I turn onto a narrow cobblestone street and find myself in front of the little store where I saw the double frame.

I stand at the window with a racing heart, hesitating, then go in.

Again, I am alone, the only customer. She is there, the proprietor, with her dust cloth, wiping a candlestick. The frame is in the same place, without photographs in it. The envelope of pictures still has not arrived, but I hold out hope. The postal strike has made a mess of things, but I've heard lots of stories about letters and packages long overdue suddenly appearing. I lift the frame, feeling its substantial weight. I hold it very close and study the delicate leafwork.

The proprietor comes near and says the same things she said to me a month before, as if time had stood still in this shop: that the frame had been in the same house many years facing out at the sea, that the sea air caused the brass to oxidize. Turning it around, I hope that since it hasn't sold, the cost might be less, but it is the same. If I spend the money on it, it will take up almost all of my savings for Yeats country.

Always when I've thought of Yeats country, I've imagined a distant, barely audible chorus of voices filling the air over Ben Bulben or Lough Gill, a chorus that portends a miracle. Now as I stand there in the shop, I hear that chorus, but there's an element of discord in it.

I feel afraid, not of the Yeats country I see in the pamphlet I hold in my hand, but of the one that lives in my imagination, the Yeats country where I expect to find redemption.

"I could have cleaned the green from the brass," the woman says. "That could have been tended to." Her hair is very white and soft like floss and her eyes behind the lit screens of her glasses are dark blue, like lapis. "But that green has a beauty, doesn't it? It's one of the things that draws you to the frame."

When she touches my shoulder, my eyes go damp. *She knows me*, I think.

"Am I right?" she asks.

When I say yes, she smiles and I am convinced for some reason that she is going to embrace me, but she remains where she is.

I imagine that she has the answer. If I ask her, she might tell me why I am afraid to go to Yeats country. She might reassure me, and whatever this notion is that is paralyzing me will let go.

"Do you want to buy it?" she asks, breaking my daze.

Without thinking I give a nod and she takes the frame from me and turns. I follow her to the cash register, where I watch her wrap it in paper and tie it with coarse string.

I can still explain that I can't really afford it. No harm has been done. She can still unwrap it. But she touched my shoulder. It matters to her that I am buying it, and I cannot bear to disappoint her. I have my most recent pay packet from Dobbins in my purse.

I leave the shop carrying my parcel and walk without direction on the cobblestone streets. I begin to wonder if Yeats country is for me what Ireland was for my father, a place outside of time, one that must remain safe in the realm of myth. Castles engulfed in mist. Hazel woods with deer that are never hunted.

•

On our way to Carlsbad Caverns in southern New Mexico, we stop at White Sands Missile Range, white drifts of sand as far as the eye can see. The wind is high. The sand crests and runs like waves. We dance in circles and roll down the peaks as Mom lifts the camera to her eye.

Sheila squats and takes a handful of the white sand. As Mom focuses and clicks, the wind blows the sand from between Sheila's fingers.

•

I put the frame on the little faux mantel in my room. Even with no pictures in it, it suggests my parents to me. The dark blue velvet backing behind each glass is scattered with minute flecks of white dust or lint, so they look like two night skies.

•

Dusk at Carlsbad Caverns, we stand in suspense with a crowd of other tourists. Bats fly out of the dark mouth of rock and ascend, like endless swarms of insects against the purple clouds.

•

I focus on auditions, trying to carve out a future for myself as an actress in the Dublin theater. I go to an audition for something that I think will be perfect for me, a play called *Hollywood B Movie*. It goes well, and afterward the director, who it turns out is from the States, takes me aside and tells me that an actress who works steadily with the company is already cast, and that most of the roles have been cast in advance and auditions are just for show. That, he tells me, is the case in many of the auditions. The Dublin theater world is a small, closed circle. Still, he says, it is good that I came. He likes my work and says he'll keep me in mind for future productions. He gives me the names of two other local directors, and I have meetings with them. If something right for me comes up, each of them says, they'll let me know.

•

I send Denis several letters and don't hear back from him. But one day in December when I come home from work, I find a blue envelope slipped under my door. It is a letter from Denis and he tells me that he thinks of me when he is thinking of other people. That everybody is compared to me. He signs it *With lots of love, Denis xxx.*

•

The night my father gave my mother the French perfume, Je Reviens, he took her to a Russian opera, *Boris Godunov,* at the Met. In the near darkness of the theater, the soft floral scent, which she'd dabbed on her throat and behind her ears, drifted sweetly between them.

•

I lie in bed in my room on Marguerite Road and close my eyes.

Pacing barefoot along a rocky ledge I wait for Denis in the late afternoon, the wind at my hair and my long, rough skirt. I look down a sweeping precipice at the tumultuous sea.

As the inland sky turns slightly purple with the descending sun, I see him coming from a path along the hill. We smile shyly at each other, then go into the cottage where we live together, and eat before the fire. Afterward, when my anticipation has reached too high a pitch, he blows out the flame in the paraffin lamp. We take off our clothes and lie facing each other, the whitewashed walls twitching softly with shadows, his face, chest, and arms lit by the glow of the waning fire.

•

Mom hangs wind chimes on the back porch. I love the melodiousness, but in states of half sleep, the chiming sounds agitated to me, music that is trying but cannot quite form.

•

I buy Christmas gifts to send back to New Mexico. Scarves for Tracy and Sheila made of fine Aran wool, a pink one and a purple one. For Jerry and Karen, a plaque for their kitchen that says: *Half a bap with sugar on the top.*

•

Just after Christmas, Letty invites me to move into an empty room in the big third-floor flat she rents on Lower Baggot Street. I jump at the chance. I'll be in the center of the city, only blocks away from Dobbins and the Focus Theatre. And I'll pay less in rent.

Letty's building is an old gray brick Georgian, four floors high, connected to a long line of similar buildings that runs the length of Lower Baggot Street. The staircases are wide, and the flat unheated, like most everywhere else in Ireland. The ceilings are very high, and stratospheres of cold hover over each room. The whole flat seems to lean, the floors and walls uneven, slightly aslant. Letty calls it "the ship on Baggot Straits."

"It's on the verge of collapse," she says with a smile the first time I come over.

"Then I know I belong here," I say and we laugh.

I write to Denis with the new address. He has not answered my last letter. I ask him again to please come to Dublin.

The room I move into is the brightest and coldest in the flat. The fittings on the enormous window that overlooks Baggot Street are ancient, so any blasts of wind racing past come in through the corners. The old, lumpy bed, which is actually a collapsed couch that Letty acquired years before "for a song," as she puts it, is a sad, worn-out thing. One side of it slopes downward, and in order not to fall off, I have to position myself in a certain dip carved out for me by the previous owner, whom I try, as I lie there, not to imagine.

•

Letty's own single bed serves also as a couch in the main room, which faces the back of the building, bare winter trees visible just outside the window. There is a kitchen area in this same room, the walls painted black. "So you don't see the dirt," Letty says, smiling.

Between the two rooms Letty's big, messy studio is crowded with various tables and armatures, sacks of plaster and buckets of wet clay under big, cloudy sheets of plastic. Dried clay streaks the walls.

Every night while living here I drink warm milk and honey and take a hot water bottle in with me to bed, where I cover myself not only with every old blanket Letty has in there but also with my clothes and my coat, and sometimes some of the canvas tarps used to cover sculptures.

In the morning Letty fires up the paraffin heater in her room, and we huddle around it, drinking instant coffee. There is no refrigerator, so she keeps a bottle of milk in a bowl of cold water. Now and then we go up Leeson Street and buy a bucket of coal, lug it back together, then light a coal fire in the grate.

•

In Tracy and Sheila's apartment in Albuquerque, the three of us drink beer and listen to the radio. We are a little tipsy when "Going to California" comes on.

We put our arms around each other and sing along:

Someone told me there's a girl out there
With love in her eyes and flowers in her hair.

When the mandolin begins to play sweetly, Sheila smiles. The edges of Tracy's face grow indistinct. Her eyes shine.

•

To make extra money I model for Letty, and for a month or so, a supine, nude, clay figure of me, which Letty is constantly wetting with splashes of water, inhabits a table in the studio.

After hours of sculpting and modeling, we walk through the park at Fitzwilliam Square, and sometimes end up at the National Gallery, looking at the Rodin sculptures, walking around them in breathless silence. I love *The Burghers of Calais*, massive distended figures concentrated with emotion, gesturing with gnarled, over-sized hands. Or we go to Doheny and Nesbitt's, a pub across Baggot Street, and drink two or three Irish coffees.

I tell Letty about Denis and show her the letter he wrote to me.

She reads it over twice. "He sounds incredibly sweet, Regina," she says. "But I don't know. I just wouldn't put that much hope in him."

"Why not?" I ask.

"He's reaching out but he's also pulling away. 'If I ever get to Dublin . . .'"

"I know," I say, wincing at the words. "But maybe there's a chance, Letty. Maybe he'll come to Dublin. If you only knew how much I want to be with him again."

She gives my forearm a sympathetic squeeze.

Why is it, I ask her, Ireland being so small across, that people speak as if getting to the other side is such a monumental endeavor, like trying to leave one world for another?

•

Letty and I stay up late and talk about ghosts. I tell her about the enchantments, how sometimes the ghosts have shadows, or I can smell them. She tells me about a time two years before when she moved into a tiny flat with her ex-boyfriend, Tony. The previous tenant had committed suicide. She awakened one night and there at her bedside was a figure of a man from the waist up, looking at her with the saddest expression she had ever seen. She did not feel afraid and reached out and touched the man's stomach and her hand went through it. The man recoiled as if he could feel her hand, and looked even sadder.

I'm amazed that she wasn't afraid and keep asking her why, but she says she doesn't know why. She just wasn't afraid.

•

I'm visiting Tracy and Sheila in Albuquerque when, on impulse, we take a drive out on the old dirt highway to the ghost town Madrid.

There's not a sign of another living soul in this town. The houses are dull brown stone and gray wood and rusted, corrugated tin. All are missing doors and windows. We park, get out, and wander, each in her own direction. The sky gathers, rumbling softly until it breaks. Rain falls inside the houses and tall dry grass grows through cracks in the floors.

Behind a rotted wood frame that was once a window I watch my sisters exploring. They go into the empty shell of a house across the dirt road, and I hear what sounds like a board falling.

"Be careful!" I cry out, and am surprised by how loudly and clearly my voice echoes.

They look over at me through an empty doorframe.

"Okay!" Sheila calls. Tracy waves.

·

We have our hot milk and honey but before we say good night I ask Letty if I can borrow her wireless radio. The talk about ghosts has me agitated.

I lie in my room in the dark with enough light coming through the window from Baggot Street below to illuminate the edges of things. I listen to broadcasts of news and music out of London and Edinburgh, sometimes breaking transmissions of Italian or Teutonic voices crackling with distance, the insomniac night world of Europe, fading in and out, dissolving awhile into static before returning, as if on tides.

·

I bolt upright in the dark. A slender ghost waits at the foot of my bed, a milky, shuddering illumination. For the split second that I remain silent, her bright face contorts in waves like a reflection in moving water.

"No!" I shout. "No!" And she rushes through the wall.

I'm in my room on Baggot Street, Letty's wireless still playing with poor, crackling reception, vague fanciful music with flutes. Where the figure was, nothing remains but a smear of light.

The doctor at the psychiatric ward asked me if the ghost at the foot of my bed in my uncle's house might have been my mother. The question had unnerved me. How could it have been, with a face so unrecognizable?

But I feel her now in that smear of light, and in the familiar burning smell left on the cold air of the room, like a dozen candles have been blown out at once.

My mother had my father's face put back together, but no one had my mother's face put back together.

The flutes on the radio are almost drowned out by a sudden hiss of white noise. My heart still races.

A day or two after my mother died, Uncle Jack came back from the funeral home, where he had tried to arrange for an open-casket wake. I heard him speaking quietly to Aunt Pat, telling her that it wasn't possible, that there was no face to put back together. It had shattered. It had been all over the room.

·

My mother moves through the room making sure my sisters are covered. She stands at the foot of my bed.

I close my eyes.

•

Spring arrives but it is still damp and frigid. Joan, a friend from the Focus, invites me along to a lively bar where we hear the Wolfe Tones singing pro-IRA songs, about the unrelenting hatred for England and the monster Oliver Cromwell. Joan knows a few people in a big group at one table and we join them.

Something about the middle-aged man sitting next to me reminds me of my father. He is of the same large build and has a similar forehead and nose. He seems very interested in the fact that I am American.

"Very few here really move forward from where they begin. I can say that to you and you'll understand because you're a Yank and you know what it means to move forward."

"I think you idealize Yanks," I say. "The Irish are a very energetic people . . ."

He shakes his head and talks about how quickly a life might pass and end in failure. "Don't let all of this fool you," he says, waving his hand to indicate the room filled with exuberance and irrepressible chatter. "Turn any corner in Dublin on a breezy day and you'll smell decay. Too many of us here are living under a curse."

The band starts up another fast-paced pro-IRA rant against "the bastards" and the man moves his head in time to the music. When the song is finished, he says, "The Irish were chieftains. We were once royalty, every one of us." His tone is nostalgic and sad.

He lives here, an Irishman in Ireland, yet he too is plagued with nostalgia, some fundamental sense of loss, and a penchant for the dramatic. Maybe that sadness is in the blood itself, born of history, centuries of tribal memory: lost battles and wars, torture, starvation, murder. Is that it, I ask him, the fall from the age of chieftains? Is that the thing that is forever lost and so longed for?

"Yes, we've lost that world," he says. "We fell from a golden age, what Yeats called 'romantic Ireland.'"

The mention of Yeats both agitates and excites me. I feel terrible guilt for having let go of my dream of Yeats country. I tell him that I intended to go there in honor of my father, who is dead, and how things keep happening to prevent it, or else I procrastinate and lose the chance. I've had a few glasses of Harp, and this man's resemblance to my father makes me speak to him in a tone too familiar for our brief acquaintance. As if I am reassuring my father, I say, "I can still try to get there. I *will* get there."

The man studies me. "It's a lovely place to visit, but what do you expect to find there?"

"I've imagined that it's a more elevated place. I don't know, a mystical place."

"Well, I understand why it is you believe that. Just look at the poetry. Yeats was a dreamer. He strained after the mystical. Don't get me wrong, I'm a great admirer of the old man, his poems about Irish history and mythology especially. But I'm among the camp that believes that Yeats's preoccupation with visions and shadow worlds was all gobbledygoop. It's a gorgeous place on the planet, but it's as real as Dublin or Brooklyn or Timbuktu."

I feel myself deflating, but still I cling to the small hope that this man, who looks like my father, will illuminate me somehow, absolve me of my negligence. "I feel I've let my father down," I say.

He asks me how my father died, and the answer comes, almost too easily, out of my mouth. "He shot himself."

He is silent for a few moments and then asks, "You're worried that *you* let *your father* down? After the unforgivable thing he did to you?"

My heart riots. "I know that Catholics think that suicide . . ."

"I'm not talking about a sin against God. I've no interest in that. Do you have siblings?"

"Yes."

He rolls his eyes. "I'm talking about a sin against his own children."

•

"The right thing to do is always to come clean," my father says. "You go to your teachers and tell them that you messed up."

He sits forward on the couch with his hands laced together. There's no anger in him that I've cut so many of my high school classes, just encouragement and a note of persuasion.

"It simplifies everything. You just tell the truth. Plus, it's the right thing to do."

I feel as if he relates to my predicament. He is giving me the right answer. There is relief in not lying or trying to hide something, relief in admitting to a mistake.

My father is a generous man, full of forgiveness.

•

I sit up in the darkness in my room in Dublin and cry because I miss my mother. I cry because my mother died without a face.

•

I walk aimlessly and find myself on O'Connell Street. I get onto a bus to Lough Bray, thirty minutes outside Dublin. Another waitress told me about it, a beautiful mountain lake with surrounding cliffs. If you are lucky, she said, while walking on the well-worn track around the water, you might see deer. She told me how easy it is to get there, and that it costs virtually nothing to go.

Walking along the trail around Lough Bray, looking for deer, I see two swans come together out of the water and walk on marshy land. The smaller one, which I assume is the female, has something red on one of her wings. At first I think it is blood, but then realize it is an area where feathers are missing and the flesh beneath is exposed.

The larger swan spreads and beats his wings; a powerful dry sound like harsh fabric brushing at harsh fabric, and the heavy creature lifts onto the air. The smaller swan watches his ascension uneasily. She moves back and forth, circles a few times and looks panicked. She seems confused as though there's been no signal between them, as if there is something wrong with his departure. The sky is so vast, it is strange when he becomes no longer visible. Worry grips me.

As a middle-aged couple holding hands strolls by, I stop them and ask, "Isn't it right that swans are monogamous and mate for life?"

They say yes, and I explain what I saw.

"Oh, he'll be back," the man says. "They don't leave each other."

And then, as if a spell has overtaken her, the female swan stretches tall, and spreads her wings. The three of us watch her. I know then that the wing with missing feathers is injured. It does not completely flex like the other. Still, she beats them both until she lifts on the air, straining her body, struggling to go in the direction he disappeared. But soon, with a great awkward flapping of the good wing, she comes down again to the ground.

"Ah, she's injured, the poor thing," the woman says.

"He'll come back, though," the man says and the two of them wander off.

I remain where I am, looking back and forth between the place in the sky where I last saw a trace of him, and the female on the ground. I want to believe he will come back, but I don't. When I look at the female walking in uneasy circles, then bellowing up at the sky, I imagine the fast, light heartbeat going within her, and then I feel it in my own stomach and chest and throat.

·

I get off the bus near O'Connell Bridge in the late afternoon, and am heading back to Baggot Street, when it begins to rain, making the dark fall early. I step into a shop on Kildare Street and purchase a box of Silk Cut cigarettes. The rain intensifies and I wait it out in the shop. There's been a lot of rain and the place retains an odor that I decide is a mixture of mildew and the slaughterhouse. It is a smell I have gotten used to, living for a year in Ireland. Pale gray sausages and raw rashers of bacon sit on a plate near the cash register and can be purchased singly. Cuts of mutton lie discoloring in a glass display case, also unrefrigerated. I light a cigarette and stand at the window, watching the gutters rush dark with rain. The past months, I've often spotted in the distance, walking on a road or standing waiting for a light to change, a man or woman of certain proportions or physical details. I wait for the man or woman to turn and look at me, expecting to see my father or my mother, peaceful, released from their earlier difficult selves, as if some compassionate deity has brought them home. After crucifixion, I have been taught since I was tiny, comes resurrection.

It amazes me that even now in my deflated state, angry and disappointed, I am doing it. A man passing on the other side of the street holding a newspaper over his head against the rain could so easily have my father's face.

It goes through my mind that maybe the ghosts that come and stand, waiting for me to face them, to look at them in their ugliness, are embodiments of the horror of my parents' deaths, which I resist accepting with every ounce of my energy.

Letty said to me that she thought that if I looked at them without flinching, they would not drive me mad. "Maybe they don't really have all the power you think they have," she said. I dismissed her words. Now the thought that this might be right shimmers within me. But that lasts only a moment. It will be years before I will be able to consider facing them.

Everything in me hurts as I walk back to Baggot Street, a hurt that leaks into my bones and viscera and skin.

I tell myself that my parents are dead, that I have to stop looking for them here, that I have to stop thinking there is some entrance in Ireland to an Otherworld. My parents' bodies are buried side by side in soldiers' graves on the green hill overlooking Rosario Boulevard in Santa Fe.

Today, the scorched grains from the Guinness Brewery
on the wind, the exhaust of buses, the deep-fried smells
from the chip and curry shops, all of which I've grown
used to, feel suddenly alien to me.

•

It is within days after the trip to Lough Bray that the
photographs arrive.

I tear the envelope open. Inside are three smaller en-
velopes. In the first one are various family pictures.

Many are blurred. My mother's camera has not cap-
tured the New Mexico light, but has filtered and drained
it of its intensity.

There is one of each of our First Communions, and
a few old black-and-whites in front of the house, Tracy
and me posing with Nanny, and a few of Jerry, Tracy,
and me with Nanny on the plaza in downtown Santa Fe.

In the second envelope there are five of just the house
surrounded by the poplars, taken from across the street,
the willow visible on the front lawn. It is a house the color
of sunflowers, or very ripe corn, though it appears in the
pictures a less vibrant shade.

From the third envelope I extract the two glossy
black-and-whites of my parents, a little creased, taken in
Yonkers or Manhattan right before they married.

Here is my father in his late twenties, a solid figure
standing in the garden of what must be a church, wearing

a brimmed felt hat, a gray coat, collar and tie visible at his neck. He smiles, his focus off to the side, and I can tell from his alert expression, both mischievous and intelligent, that he is about to say something that will make my mother laugh.

Here is my mother, taken in the same garden, probably on the same overcast day, but at closer range. She wears a dark coat, her wavy, windblown hair parted at the side, a playful flash of sarcasm in her warm smile. She is sitting on a low wall, one hand resting on her lap, a cigarette poised between two gloved fingers.

Both pictures are fragile, almost weightless. The longer I look at my parents' faces, the less I can see them, and soon it is as though I am not looking at anything.

I put the pictures back in the envelope. Leaving it on the bed, I go out and walk to the city center, where I wander in and out of the shops on Grafton Street, then stop for coffee in Bewley's Oriental Café, popular and overcrowded, a massive, daylit room under a cloud of cigarette smoke. I sit at one of the carved dark polished wood booths along the wall, sipping hot coffee and finding refuge in the high bedlam of chatter, hissing tea urns, forks and knives clattering on porcelain.

I keep thinking of the pictures, wishing I had placed the large envelope that held them under some books or weighted it down with something. Why do I wish this, I wonder, and laugh a little over it. Do I think I'll come back and find all the photos floating in the air near the ceiling?

•

I sit with the envelope of pictures on my lap. I cannot bring myself to take out the black-and-whites of my youthful parents. Instead, I extract the ones my mother took of the house. Three of the pictures are older. They have no dates written on them, but the trees are not as tall and the car on the driveway is one from when I was younger. The other two pictures are dated September 1974, the month my mother died. In one, the trees have grown so high, they cannot be seen all the way to the top. The willow, too, is enormous.

The other picture, an incomplete close-up of the house, is taken from the front lawn, not across the street like the others. When I first looked at it earlier in the day, I did not see what I see now: my mother's shadow. For a few moments, I have the feeling that it's going to disappear, but the longer I look, the more certain it becomes.

She must have been standing on the lawn with the willow and the poplars behind her. I know from the red cast to the light that it is dusk. Her shadow is aslant on the wall of the house, arms high, elbows akimbo as she holds the camera, her legs elongated on the grass before her and on the porch. The shadows of the poplars, less distinct, lean at the same angle behind her.

How could I not have seen her shadow earlier? It seems so apparent to me now. And then, almost impossibly, I see something else, barely discernible in the grainy dark of the kitchen window: my sisters peering out.

My father is five months dead, my brother off with his friends. And me, where am I? My absence in this picture chills me, it is so palpable. And now again, here I am, on another continent, a world away from my sisters and my brother. I miss them with an awful urgency, a yawning ache in my chest and stomach. It is time, now, to go back.

I look at the other picture from the month my mother died, taken from a distance, the poplars so unnaturally tall. I think of my mother watering them for hours on weekends, and in the evenings after work. I hear the rushing sound they made in the wind, awkward giants, bending and gesturing, never easy in the desert air.

ACKNOWLEDGMENTS

I owe enormous gratitude to Masie Cochran, my brilliant, intuitive editor whose vision and passion for *Ghost Songs* has never flagged. Heartfelt thanks, too, to my agents, Ellen Levine and Alexa Stark at Trident Media Group, for believing in this memoir and so tirelessly working on its behalf. I owe so much to everyone at Tin House Books: Nanci McCloskey, Diane Chonette, Meg Cassidy, Sabrina Wise, Meg Storey. Much gratitude also to Anne Horowitz.

Thanks are owed to many people who have contributed feedback and/or support during the slow evolution of this book: Tracy Handley, Jane Lury, Scott Stephens, Hope Brennan, Rita Gabis, Jenna Johnson, Joy Harris, Sarah Twombly, Terra Chalberg, Bill Clegg, and Thom Taylor.

Deepest gratitude of all goes to my husband, Neil, and my daughter, Miranda. I am so privileged to share my life with you both.

Book Club Questions:

Ghost Songs is brimming with stories from Regina's childhood. Which flashbacks were the most memorable for you? Which were the most shocking, the most hopeful, the happiest?

Do you believe in the ghosts in *Ghost Songs* or do you chalk Regina's visions up to posttraumatic stress and grief?

Regina begins her memoir remembering a time at a college party when two actors called her Lady Ophelia. Why do you think she opens with this story, and how does it set the stage for the rest of the memoir?

Oceans play an important role in *Ghost Songs*. What impact does the move to the dry landscape of New Mexico have on Regina and her family?

What did Regina's parents feel about Ireland, the country they'd never been to? Why does Regina move to Ireland? What does she hope to find there?

What does Yeats Country mean to Regina? Do you wish she had made it there? Why? Why do you think she didn't go?

Describe Regina's relationship to her siblings and discuss the role they played in one another's lives.

What character traits—both positive and negative—do you think Regina inherited from her parents? And how do you think those traits shaped her early adulthood?

What does the title *Ghost Songs* mean to you?

Despite her grief, it never feels as though Regina blames her parents. Were you able to be equally nonjudgmental?

The cover of *Ghost Songs* is a photograph from Regina's parents' wedding day. How does this photograph and the art around it make you feel?

© NSJPHOTO.COM

REGINA McBRIDE is the author of four novels and one book of poetry and the recipient of fellowships from the National Endowment for the Arts and the New York Foundation for the Arts. She is an adjunct professor of English at Hunter College in New York City, where she teaches creative writing.